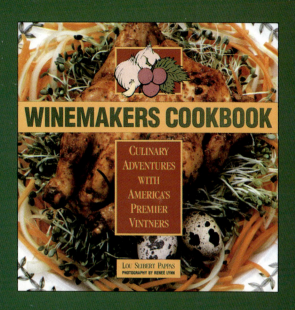

WINEMAKERS COOKBOOK

CULINARY
ADVENTURES
WITH
AMERICA'S
PREMIER
VINTNERS

LOU SEIBERT PAPPAS
PHOTOGRAPHY BY RENÉE LYNN

Printed in Japan by Toppan Printing
Co., Ltd., Tokyo.

Library of Congress Cataloging-in-
Publication Data

Pappas, Lou Seibert.
    Winemakers cookbook.

    Includes index.
    1. Cookery. 2. Menus. 3. Vintners –
    California.
    I. Title.
    TX715.P1954 1986   641.5   86-17603
    ISBN 0-87701-373-X

Design: Dare Porter/Graphic Design,
            San Francisco

Composition: On Line Typography

Illustration: Marilyn Hill

Distributed in Canada by
Raincoast Books
112 East 3rd Avenue
Vancouver, B.C.
V5T 1C8

10 9 8 7 6 5 4 3 2 1

Chronicle Books
One Hallidie Plaza
San Francisco, CA

TABLE OF CONTENTS

INTRODUCTION

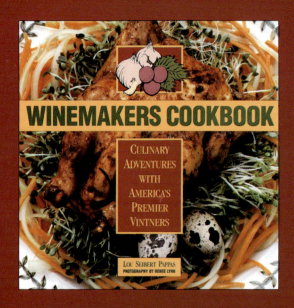

Vintners are a special breed. Dauntless in their pursuit of excellence, theirs is a dedicated career.

The former endeavors of these men and women represent a varied cross section. Among them is a lawyer, fireman, ballet dancer, tire tycoon, artist, venture capitalist, builder, and bread merchant. Only a few have grown up with a family heritage of wine making. Lessons learned in previous careers and versatile talents provide useful stepping-stones for the "hats of many feathers" they wear today.

This is a hard-working, persevering group. All own their own wineries. Though some have joined family enterprises, other pooled their own resources and created boot-strap operations. In tandem with the production of their wine, they face its marketing, which often involves day-to-day public relations and constant travel.

The reward of endless labor is the pleasure of savoring vintages with family and friends at a table brimming with prime local bounty.

Menus are chosen with care, in tune with the season. Informality prevails, except when a chef is on hand for a catered party. Time is at a premium and dishes are achieved with ease and aplomb. Family heritage plays a leitmotiv throughout, as international foods are re-created for guests and holiday occasions.

Gardens provide choice seasonal vegetables, herbs, and flowers in abundance, both for edible garnish and table decoration.

A refreshing salad is likely dressed with extra-virgin olive oil or a rich nut oil and just a splash of vinegar, perhaps balsamic, raspberry, or a vintner's own herb-scented wine vinegar. Or lemon juice may provide a piquant accent. They know to tone down the acid, so their vintages will shine through with clarity.

The meal may star lamb, beef, pork, or poultry raised by a neighboring rancher, or the region's game, such as quail, pheasant, or boar. When salmon is running, it is a favored fish to grill over mesquite or bake and mate with premium Chardonnays and Cabernets.

Fruits from local orchards often pair with cheese—Brie, mascarpone, or California chèvre—for dessert. Or crispy nut wafers or butter cookies may complement a fruit sorbet or freshly churned ice cream.

Entertaining goes on almost around the clock: a Sunday brunch, a midday picnic, luncheon under the apple tree or in the arbor. Dinner comes at dusk in the garden, canopied by oaks, or beside the barrels in the cool of the aging room.

The warmth, camaraderie, and sincerity that accompanies the wines and party fare make for countless memorable occasions. Here two dozen vintner owners of the 662 bonded California wineries each share two menus for triumphant entertaining.

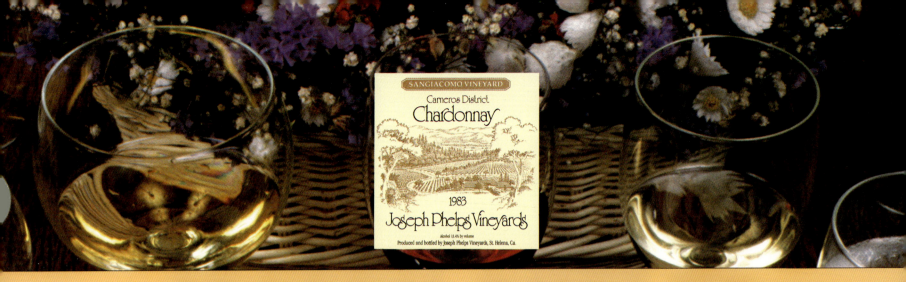

JOSEPH PHELPS VINEYARDS

Joseph Phelps leads a multi-faceted life. Builder, vintner, and grocer, he is also a superb, creative cook.

A Coloradan with a successful career in construction, he built wineries for others, then in 1974 decided to build one for himself. It is nestled in Spring Valley, east of St. Helena, on 670 acres long known as Connolly Ranch.

Here stands an architecturally striking wooden cellar— actually two pavilions joined by a closed bridge. Stainless-steel fermenters, oak tanks, casks, and barrels fill the pavilions. The bridge houses offices and a laboratory. A wood-paneled reception room seats sixty for a special dinner.

The winery adjoins a spacious quarry-tiled kitchen with an eight-burner gas range and stainless-steel counters. Guests are entertained informally at a long French-style pine table that runs down the center of the room.

Joe occasionally presides over the skillet, perhaps to turn out one of his own creations like glazed shallots and shiitakes. This dish might introduce a four-course guest luncheon partnered by a quartet of world-class vintages.

The kitchen is also where the crew dinners are prepared, now by a professional chef, often a recent graduate of San Francisco's California Culinary Academy. Until a few years ago, Joe himself was at the big black range daily, cooking *stifatho,* lasagna, or ham hocks for the night and day shifts of twenty or more workers.

An expansive garden produces bushels of vegetables and herbs, especially basil. "I don't feel secure

unless I have a half acre of it," Joe says with a laugh.

An innovative cook, he enjoys getting dinner together "with what's on hand in the refrigerator that strikes a responsive chord in me."

His blond, vivacious wife Pat assures that, "Joe has fun in the kitchen. It is his pleasure. He has a lot of respect for the ingredients."

A master at pairing wine with food, he has a keen sense for cooking with it. "My preference is to use less wine as a ingredient during warm-weather months," he explains. "I am inclined to use more in recipes for cold-weather dishes like hearty stews or rich desserts.

"In general, I'd advise following simple rules, avoid being too fussy, and choose whichever wine seems most compatible with the food you are cooking. Food comes first and the wine should enhance, never overpower, the flavor of the dish," he cautions.

A passion for fine food prompted Joe to purchase Oakville Grocery, a century-old country store. Today, after a thorough restocking, it is Napa Valley's gourmet center, brimming with exotic imported and local condiments and beautiful fresh produce.

For Joe, becoming a vintner is traveling "full circle." His family was involved in agriculture before turning to construction. He also started making wine at home in Denver in the late sixties. "I bought grapes from Bob Ellsworth's The Compleat Winemaker, shipped from right here in St. Helena." The fermenting took place in his fallout shelter.

Today he leans on the skill of wine maker Craig Williams and marketing vice-president Bruce Neyers. Joe himself is praised for his managerial skills, as he encourages his employees to grow and develop their own potential.

As vintner and dedicated cook, Joe sets forth a menu that appeals to all senses. Artistic yet simply prepared, the plates reflect the touch of a person with a sincere love of food and wine.

MENU
Catered by Suzanne McDowell

JOSEPH PHELPS GEWÜRTRAMINER

•

SAUTÉ OF SHALLOTS AND
SHIITAKE MUSHROOMS*
JOSEPH PHELPS ZINFANDEL, NAPA

•

SALMON FILLETS IN GRAPE LEAVES
WITH RAISIN SAUCE*
SPINACH SAUTÉ
ROASTED NEW POTATOES*
JOSEPH PHELPS CHARDONNAY

•

BLACK CURRANT TEA ICE CREAM WITH
TRUFFLES*
JOSEPH PHELPS SCHEUREBE
LATE HARVEST

Sauté of Shallots and Shiitake Mushrooms
3 tablespoons unsalted butter
½ cup marble-size whole shallot bulbs, peeled and trimmed
2 cups fresh shiitake mushrooms (about ⅓ pound), stems removed and caps cut crosswise into ½-inch-wide strips
1 teaspoon balsamic vinegar
3 tablespoons glace de viande, or 6 tablespoons demi-glace
Salt and freshly ground black pepper to taste
2 tablespoons chopped fresh Italian (flat leaf) parsley, cilantro, or curly parsley

In a large skillet, heat butter over medium-high heat until slightly browned. Reduce heat, add shallots, and sauté 7 to 10 minutes, or until golden brown. Add mushrooms and sauté until soft, about 2 to 3 minutes. Add vinegar and glace de viande, stirring to blend. Season with salt and pepper. Spoon onto individual serving plates and sprinkle with parsley. Makes 4 servings.

Salmon Fillets in Grape Leaves with Raisin Sauce
2 tablespoons golden raisins
3 tablespoons fresh lemon juice
6 tablespoons extra-virgin olive oil
Pinch each granulated sugar and salt
8 to 12 bottled grape leaves
4 salmon fillets (6 ounces each)

Plump the raisins in water to cover. Drain raisins, put into a small bowl, and stir in lemon juice, oil, sugar, and salt; set aside. Remove stems from grape leaves and rinse leaves under cold running water. Overlap 2 or 3 leaves on a work surface, shiny side down, place a salmon fillet in the center, and wrap leaves around fillet, encasing it completely. Repeat with remaining leaves and fillets.

Grill salmon packets over a medium-hot mesquite fire, turning once, until barely cooked through, about 4 minutes. Place salmon packets on individual plates and spoon raisin sauce over the top. Makes 4 servings.

Roasted New Potatoes
12 small new potatoes
2 tablespoons olive oil
Salt to taste
½ teaspoon dried thyme, crumbled
2 cloves garlic, minced

Place potatoes in an oven-proof pan with oil, salt, thyme, and garlic; stir to coat potatoes. Cover pan and bake in a preheated 400° F. oven for 40 minutes, or until cooked through. Stir several times during cooking. Makes 4 servings.

Black Currant Tea Ice Cream with Truffles
2 cups milk
½ cup black currant tea leaves
8 egg yolks
1 cup granulated sugar
2 cups whipping cream
Truffles (see Basic Recipes)

In a saucepan, scald the milk and remove from the heat. Place tea leaves in a tea ball or tie in cheesecloth and add to saucepan; let steep 3 to 4 minutes and remove tea.

Beat egg yolks until light and beat in sugar. Pour in hot tea-flavored milk and stir to blend. Turn into the top pan of a double boiler and cook over simmering water, stirring, until custard coats a spoon, about 10 minutes. Cool custard by nesting the pan in a bowl of ice. Stir in cream and refrigerate until well chilled.

Prepare the Truffles. Pour the custard into an ice-cream freezer and freeze according to manufacturer's instructions. Spoon ice cream into dessert bowls (it should be slightly soft for best flavor and texture) and scatter 4 to 5 Truffles over each serving. Makes 6 to 8 servings, about 1¾ quarts.

MENU

Catered by Suzanne McDowell

CHÈVRE SOUFFLÉ*
JOSEPH PHELPS CHARDONNAY
SANGIACOMO

•

GRILLED PORK LOIN*
ROASTED BELL PEPPERS
GRILLED LEEKS WITH
MUSTARD CREAM*
JOSEPH PHELPS ZINFANDEL,
ALEXANDER VALLEY

•

PAPAYA FAN AND LIME SEGMENTS
SCHEUREBE*
JOSEPH PHELPS SCHEUREBE SPECIAL
SELECT LATE HARVEST

Chèvre Soufflé

1½ cups milk
1 cup whipping cream
6 tablespoons unsalted butter
5 tablespoons all-purpose flour
½ teaspoon salt
¼ teaspoon each freshly ground black pepper and freshly grated nutmeg
Pinch ground cayenne pepper
5 egg yolks
7 ounces chèvre
1 cup egg whites (about 8)

2 bunches watercress, stems removed
Vinaigrette (see Basic Recipes)
12 sun-dried tomatoes, thinly sliced

Pour the milk and cream into a saucepan and scald over medium heat. In a separate saucepan, melt the butter, stir in the flour, and cook, stirring, for 2 to 3 minutes. Stir the hot milk mixture into the butter-flour mixture and bring to a boil; lower the heat slightly and cook until thickened, about 5 minutes.

Add salt, pepper, nutmeg, and cayenne and remove from the heat.

Beat egg yolks until light. Stir in the warm cream sauce and about half of the chèvre, broken into pieces. Beat egg whites until soft peaks form and fold into yolk mixture with remaining chèvre, broken into pieces. Spoon into a buttered 12-inch oval platter with 2-inch sides or into a 2-quart soufflé dish. Bake in a preheated 450° F. oven for 15 minutes, or until well browned and set.

While soufflé is baking, prepare the Vinaigrette and toss the watercress in it. To serve, arrange the watercress on individual serving plates and top with a serving of the soufflé. Surround with slices of sun-dried tomato. Makes 6 to 8 servings.

Grilled Pork Loin

¼ cup granulated sugar
2 tablespoons salt
8 each coriander seeds, black peppercorns, and lightly crushed juniper berries

1 teaspoon dried thyme, crumbled
4 quarts water
1 pork loin (about 4 pounds), boned and tied

In a large crock, combine sugar, salt, coriander seeds, peppercorns, juniper berries, thyme, and water. Immerse pork loin in this brine, holding it in place with a heavy plate, and refrigerate for 24 to 48 hours.

Remove meat from brine and pat dry. Insert a meat thermometer in the thickest portion of the loin and grill loin over a medium-hot mesquite fire, turning, about 1¼ to 1½ hours, or until thermometer registers about 160° F. Alternatively, grill in a covered barbecue about 1 hour. Makes 6 to 8 servings.

Grilled Leeks with Mustard Cream

Mustard Cream (recipe follows)
12 to 16 leeks
Olive oil
Salt and freshly ground black pepper to taste

Prepare the Mustard Cream and set aside. Split leeks lengthwise, wash thoroughly, and pat dry. Brush with oil and season with salt and pepper. Grill over a medium-hot mesquite fire until cooked through, turning, about 10 minutes. Serve with Mustard Cream, spooned over the top. Makes 6 to 8 servings.

Mustard Cream Beat together until smooth 6 tablespoons butter, at room temperature, 1 tablespoon Dijon-style mustard, and ¼ cup whipping cream.

Papaya Fan and Lime Segments Scheurebe

3 limes
½ cup water
3 tablespoons granulated sugar
1 cup Scheurebe Late Harvest
3 papayas, peeled, seeded, and thinly sliced

Cut peel, avoiding any white membrane, from 1 or more of the limes and cut into julienne to measure 2 tablespoons. In a small saucepan, bring water and 2 tablespoons sugar to a boil, stirring to dissolve sugar. Add the peel, boil for 1 minute, drain, and set aside.

Peel all of the limes and section the fruit, removing any white membrane. In a saucepan, combine the wine and remaining 1 tablespoon sugar and heat to simmering. Add lime segments and heat through. To serve, arrange a fan of papaya slices on each dessert plate. Spoon the hot lime segments over the papaya, and scatter lime peel over the top. Makes 6 servings.

FREEMARK ABBEY

1983

NAPA VALLEY
CHARDONNAY

PRODUCED AND BOTTLED BY
FREEMARK ABBEY WINERY, ST. HELENA, CALIFORNIA, U.S.A.
Alcohol 13.7% by volume

FREEMARK ABBEY
WINERY

The barbecued ribs are spicy and succulent, with an irresistible flavor that keeps calling for one more morsel. Those are Chuck Carpy's ribs, a famous specialty in St. Helena. As a partner in Freemark Abbey Winery, he is used to grilling ribs for one hundred or more at the winery's parties. At home the crispy glazed meat may accompany an outdoor buffet set forth by his talented wife, Ann.

With five almost full-grown children, she has had lots of experience preparing big family dinners. Fortunately, she loves to cook, along with a variety of other pastimes like painting, strumming the ukulele, playing bridge, and writing poetry and humorous monologues.

For family or guests, Chuck does the barbecuing, be it ribs, steaks, or whole salmon. "The rib sauce recipe is from a buddy and I've been making it for thirty-five years," says Chuck. Lately he shares the grilling task with his youngest son, Charles.

"Casual is my style," says Ann, and "usually it is dinner. Likely if people are here for wine, they stay on for dinner.

"We're a family that loves games. We play trivia, dominoes, bridge, chess, or poker and in the winter have a one-thousand-piece jigsaw puzzle set up. When guests are here we usually end up singing or playing charades."

Chuck, a native of St. Helena, carries on the family traditions of wine making, banking, and commitment to civic affairs. His namesake grandfather, Charles

Carpy, came to California from Bordeaux at the end of the Civil War.

At various times the senior Charles Carpy owned Uncle Sam Cellars in Napa, Pacific Winery in San Jose, and finally Greystone Cellars (now Christian Brothers) in St. Helena, which he sold in 1896 to go into banking in San Francisco. Chuck's father, Albert, was also a banker.

Chuck received a bachelor's degree in agricultural economics from University of California, Davis and a master's degree from Montana State University. He became a grape grower in 1961, and with several partners

founded Freemark Abbey in 1967, heading the administrative and vineyard aspects. He is a founder of the Napa National Bank and a moving force in many wine associations.

The foundations of the winery itself go back to 1875, when a retired sea captain began developing the vineyards. The property passed through several hands, devastated by phylloxera and Prohibition.

The traditional stone building that now houses the ultramodern fermenting cellar was built at the turn of the century. The partners have since added two more structures for bottling and barrel aging their wine.

Ann grew up in Berkeley and majored in art there at the University of California. She has a studio and does pastels when she finds the time.

The Carpys look to an international range of cultures for their menus. "We love ethnic food, particularly Chinese, Japanese, Greek, Mexican, and Indian," enthuses Ann. "Our cooking adventures often revolve around these cuisines."

MENU

PRAWNS WITH COCKTAIL SAUCE
RAW VEGETABLE PLATTER
WITH DILL DIP
FREEMARK ABBEY
JOHANNISBERG RIESLING

•

CHUCK'S BARBECUED SPARERIBS*
SPICY KIDNEY BEANS*
CORN ON THE COB
GARLIC FRENCH BREAD
SLICED TOMATOES
WITH MINT DRESSING
FREEMARK ABBEY
PETITE SIRAH

•

APPLE PIE À LA MODE

Chuck's Barbecued Spareribs

2 cups ketchup
¾ cup tomato purée
½ teaspoon ground cumin
4 drops liquid smoke
½ cup firmly packed brown sugar
¼ cup cider vinegar
¼ teaspoon dried basil, crumbled
2 cloves garlic, minced
1½ teaspoons chili powder
6 to 8 pounds pork spareribs, cracked

In a saucepan, combine the ketchup, tomato purée, cumin, liquid smoke, sugar, vinegar, basil, garlic, and chili powder and heat, stirring, until sugar dissolves. Remove from the heat.

Grill spareribs over a medium-hot fire for 1 hour, turing once and basting with sauce during the last 15 minutes of cooking. Serve remaining sauce in a bowl at the table. Makes 8 servings.

Spicy Kidney Beans

2 slices bacon, diced
1 medium-size onion, chopped
2 cloves garlic, minced
1 can (16 ounces) tomatoes, with liquid
1½ teaspoons Worcestershire sauce
1½ tablespoons brown sugar
1 tablespoon chopped fresh cilantro
Dash ground cayenne pepper
¼ teaspoon salt
1 small dried red chili pepper, crushed
4 cups cooked red kidney beans, or 2 cans (15½ ounces each) red kidney beans, drained

In a large saucepan, fry bacon until crisp; remove from the pan with a slotted utensil and drain on paper towels. In the drippings remaining in the pan, sauté onion and garlic until transparent, about 5 minutes. Add tomatoes and their liquid, Worcestershire sauce, sugar, cilantro, cayenne, salt, and chili pepper, cover the pan, and simmer for 30 minutes. Add beans and reserved bacon, cover, and simmer for 1 hour longer. If desired, prepare a day in advance and reheat. Makes 8 servings.

MENU

OYSTERS ON THE HALF SHELL
BLUE COSTELLO CHEESE
WITH ARMENIAN CRACKER BREAD
FREEMARK ABBEY CHARDONNAY

•

GRILLED BUTTERFLIED LEG OF LAMB
GRILLED EGGPLANTS, RED PEPPERS,
AND TORPEDO ONIONS*
PILAFF
YELLOW CROOKNECK SQUASH
WITH LEMON BUTTER*
GREEN SALAD
WITH AVOCADO AND PINK GRAPEFRUIT
FREEMARK ABBEY
CABERNET SAUVIGNON

•

PAPAYA HALVES WITH LEMON SHERBET
FREEMARK ABBEY EDELWEIN

Grilled Eggplants, Red Peppers, and Torpedo Onions

¼ pound (½ cup) butter
1 small onion, chopped
2 cloves garlic, minced
¼ cup dry white wine
¾ cup olive oil
Juice of 3 lemons
1 tablespoon chopped fresh basil, or
  1 teaspoon dried basil, crumbled
4 Japanese eggplants
3 large red bell peppers
3 torpedo onions

For the basting sauce, melt the butter in a skillet, and sauté onion and garlic over medium heat until transparent, about 5 minutes. Remove from the heat and mix in wine, oil, lemon juice, and basil. Slice unpeeled eggplants in half lengthwise. Quarter peppers lengthwise and remove seeds. Slice torpedo onions into ¾-inch-thick rounds. Dip vegetables in basting sauce and grill over a medium-hot fire on one side for 5 to 10 minutes. Turn vegetables over and continue to grill until cooked through, basting once. Transfer vegetables to a serving dish and brush them with the sauce. Makes 8 servings.

Yellow Crookneck Squash with Lemon Butter

8 to 10 yellow crook-neck squash
4 tablespoons butter
2 green onions, chopped
2 tablespoons fresh lemon juice
1 teaspoon Dijon-style mustard
1 teaspoon Worcester-shire sauce
¼ teaspoon salt
Dash freshly ground black pepper

Slice squash ½ inch thick and steam until crisp-tender, about 10 minutes. While squash are cooking, combine butter, green onions, lemon juice, mustard, Worcestershire sauce, salt, and pepper in a small saucepan. Heat just until butter melts. Transfer cooked squash slices to a serving casserole and spoon butter sauce over them. Makes 8 servings.

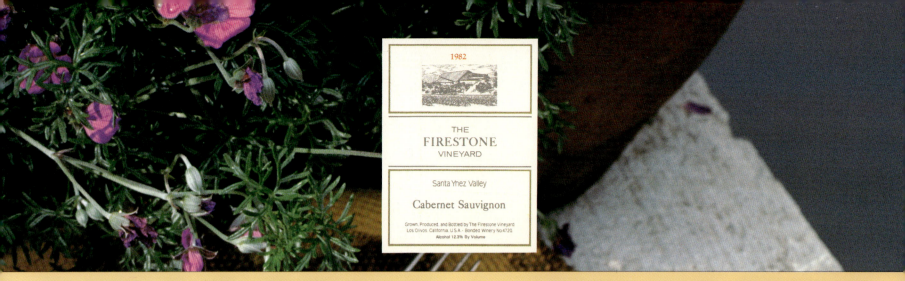

1982

THE
FIRESTONE
VINEYARD

Santa Ynez Valley

Cabernet Sauvignon

Grown, Produced, and Bottled by The Firestone Vineyard
Los Olivos, California, U.S.A. · Bonded Winery No.4720
Alcohol 12.3% By Volume

FIRESTONE VINEYARDS

A tire tycoon and a ballerina turn vintners? That's right. A. Brooks Firestone, grandson of Harvey Firestone of the rubber-tire empire, and his wife Kate, a former solo dancer with London's Royal Ballet, knew nothing about grapes when they arrived in the Santa Ynez Valley in 1973 to run a 275-acre vineyard and a 2,300-acre cattle ranch.

They studied wine making furiously, became enamored with it, and now oversee production and marketing of the seventy-five thousand cases of wine annually. "Someday," says Brooks with an amiably boyish grin, "someday, when you think of Firestone, you'll think of wine, not tires."

Beside him, willowy Kate, a pretty brunette, concurs. Already she is known as an expert on presenting superb meals matched to Firestone vintages.

A Calcutta-born daughter of an English clergyman, she met Brooks backstage in Covent Garden when he was directing the Firestone office in London. Shortly after that they married, and Brooks became the classic "executive dropout."

B rooks's father, Leonard K. Firestone, a former ambassador to Belgium, asked him to look into the investment potential of a large parcel of vineyard land he had purchased in the Santa

Ynez Valley. The investigation showed there was an overabundance of table-grape growers in California and Brooks suggested producing wine.

Intrigued by the wine business and the opportunity to pioneer a new wine region, Brooks formed the winery in an equal partnership with his father, and Suntory Limited Company of Japan. As chief executive, Brooks oversees all vineyard and winery

functions and Kate plays an active roll in public relations and marketing. They also have raised four children: Hayley is a teacher, Adam is in law school, Polly is studying drama in London, and Andrew is in grammar school.

Firestone Vineyards relies on two industry experts to maintain its high standards. One is André Tchelistcheff, the dean of California wine making, who serves as a consultant. The second is wine maker Alison Green, a graduate in oenology from the University of California, Davis.

The winery is a four-level cathedral-like structure of redwood with stained-glass windows and red-tile floors. Around the fountain in the courtyard, Kate holds classical-music concerts. The couple is extremely active in various organizations and committees devoted to the arts, politics, wine, and food.

T he Firestones are tireless champions of wine, and have injected the spirit of wholesomeness, happiness, endless energy, and elegance into the day-to-day life of farming, cattle raising, and wine production.

MENU

BARBECUED SWEETBREADS,
WILD BOAR SAUSAGE, AND
JALAPEÑO SAUSAGE WITH
A CHOICE OF MUSTARDS
FIRESTONE ROSÉ OF CABERNET

•

LAMB KEBABS WITH
YOGURT-MINT SAUCE*
WINE PILAFF*
SPINACH AND RICOTTA IN FILO*
SLICED TOMATOES, RED ONIONS,
GREEN AND RED BELL PEPPERS,
CUCUMBERS, BROCCOLI, AND
ARTICHOKES IN VINAIGRETTE
BRAIDED GREEK BREAD WITH
SWEET BUTTER
FIRESTONE PINOT NOIR

•

FRUIT PLATE WITH SHORTBREAD
FIRESTONE SELECT HARVEST RIESLING

Lamb Kebabs with Yogurt-Mint Sauce

1 cup dry white wine
½ cup olive oil
1 teaspoon salt
3 tablespoons chopped fresh rosemary, or 2 teaspoons dried rosemary, crumbled
2 cloves garlic, minced
2 pounds boneless leg of lamb, cut into 1½-inch cubes
1 pound fresh mushrooms (1½ inches in diameter), ends trimmed flush to caps
Yogurt-Mint Sauce (recipe follows)

For the marinade, combine the wine, oil, salt, rosemary, and garlic in a large bowl. Add meat and marinate at least 2 hours at room temperature. Prepare the Yogurt-Mint Sauce. Thread the meat chunks on skewers, alternating them with mushrooms. Grill skewers over a medium-hot fire, turning frequently and brushing often with marinade, until lamb is medium-rare. Serve with Yogurt-Mint Sauce. Makes 8 servings.

Yogurt-Mint Sauce

In a mixing bowl, stir together 1 pint (2 cups) plain yogurt, 2 teaspoons chopped fresh mint, 1 tablespoon fresh lemon juice, ½ teaspoon salt, and 1 teaspoon granulated sugar. Refrigerate until serving time.

Spinach and Ricotta in Filo

3 bunches fresh spinach, finely chopped, or 3 packages (10 ounces each) frozen chopped spinach, thawed
1 large onion, chopped
3 tablespoons olive oil
1 pint (16 ounces) ricotta cheese
2 eggs, beaten
½ cup freshly grated Parmesan cheese
½ teaspoon freshly grated nutmeg
Salt and freshly ground black pepper to taste
12 filo sheets (about ½ pound)
¼ pound (½ cup) butter, melted

Squeeze out any excess water from chopped spinach. In a large skillet, sauté onion in oil until transparent, about 5 minutes. Add spinach and cook gently 2 minutes. Remove from the heat and stir in ricotta, eggs, Parmesan, nutmeg, salt, and pepper.

Layer 6 filo sheets on the bottom of a greased 9-by-13-inch baking dish, brushing each sheet with melted butter as you put it into the dish. Keep remaining filo covered with a damp towel so that it doesn't dry out. Spoon spinach mixture into the filo-lined dish. Top spinach mixture with 6 more filo sheets, brushing each with melted butter. Place in a preheated 360° F. oven for 50 minutes, or until filo is golden brown. Remove from the oven, cut into squares, and serve hot or at room temperature. Makes 12 servings.

Wine Pilaff

3 tablespoons butter
1 large onion, chopped
2 cups long-grain white rice
3 cups chicken stock
1 cup dry white wine
Salt to taste
½ cup dried currants
½ cup chopped blanched almonds
½ teaspoon ground cinnamon
¼ teaspoon each freshly grated nutmeg and ground cloves

In a large saucepan, melt the butter, add onion, and sauté until transparent, about 5 minutes. Add rice and sauté just to coat grains. Add stock, wine, and salt and bring to a boil. Lower the heat, cover, and simmer for approximately 12 minutes. Add currants, almonds, cinnamon, nutmeg, and cloves. Cover and continue to cook until all the liquid is absorbed, about 8 to 10 minutes longer. Fluff with a fork before serving. Makes 8 servings.

MENU

ROASTED PISTACHIOS AND
CALIFORNIA GREEN OLIVES
FIRESTONE GEWÜRZTRAMINER
OR CHAMPAGNE

•

GREEN PEA SOUP WITH MINT*
FIRESTONE GEWÜRZTRAMINER

•

SALMON ROSÉ EN CROÛTE*
GREEN BEAN BUNDLES
FIRESTONE ROSÉ OF CABERNET

•

BIBB LETTUCE, RADICCHIO, ARUGULA,
MUSHROOMS, AND WALNUTS
IN RASPBERRY VINAIGRETTE
MONTRACHET WITH WATER BISCUITS
FIRESTONE MERLOT

•

COFFEE DEMITASSES*
FIRESTONE AMBASSADORS VINEYARD
RIESLING

Green Pea Soup with Mint

3 cups shelled fresh peas, or 2 packages (10 ounces each) frozen petite peas
4 cups chicken stock
½ cup dry white wine
1 large onion, chopped
2 tablespoons butter
2 tablespoons chopped fresh mint
Salt and freshly ground black pepper to taste
½ cup dry white wine
Mint sprigs for garnish
Sour cream or plain yogurt for garnish

In a large saucepan, cook peas in chicken stock over medium heat for 15 to 20 minutes, or until very soft. In a skillet, melt the butter, add onion, and sauté until transparent, about 5 minutes. Add onion to peas and season with mint, salt, and pepper.

Transfer pea mixture to a blender or a food processor fitted with a metal blade and purée until smooth. Pour purée into a saucepan, add wine, and heat to serving temperature. Ladle into bowls and garnish with mint and a dollop of sour cream. Makes 8 servings.

Salmon Rosé en Croûte

1 package (10 ounces) frozen puff pastry
1¾ pounds salmon fillets
Sweet mustard
Chopped fresh dill
Salt to taste
1 egg, beaten
Rosé Grape Sauce (recipe follows)

Thaw pastry in the refrigerator. On a lightly floured board, roll out pastry into a large, very thin rectangle. Cut the rectangle into 6 pieces each about 5 to 6 inches square. (If your work space is not large enough to accommodate a large rectangle, divide the pastry in half and roll out in 2 batches.) Cut salmon fillets into 6 equal portions. Spread one side of a salmon portion with mustard, place on one-half of a pastry square, coated side down, and spread top side of fish with mustard. Sprinkle fish with dill and salt. Moisten edges of pastry with water, fold uncovered half over fish, and seal edges by pressing together firmly. Repeat with remaining pastry squares and salmon. Arrange pastry packets on a baking sheet. Prick each one with fork tines and then brush tops with beaten egg. Bake packets in a preheated 425° F. oven for 15 minutes, or until golden.

Meanwhile, prepare the Rosé Grape Sauce. To serve, spoon sauce on plates, top with a hot fish pastry, and decorate serving with reserved grapes. Makes 6 servings.

Rosé Grape Sauce In a saucepan, melt 2 tablespoons butter and stir in 1 cup Rosé of Cabernet or other fruity rosé wine. Blend 1 tablespoon fresh lemon juice with 1 tablespoon cornstarch and stir into wine mixture. Add ½ teaspoon granulated sugar and ¼ teaspoon salt. Simmer to reduce and thicken, stirring frequently. Halve all but a handful of grapes from ½ pound seedless red grapes and add to the sauce just before serving. Use reserved grapes for garnish.

Coffee Demitasses

1 cup whipping cream
1¼ cups milk
½ cup granulated sugar
3 tablespoons decaffeinated instant-coffee granules
1½ teaspoons vanilla extract
6 egg yolks
Chocolate Cups (see Basic Recipes)
¼ cup coffee-flavored liqueur
Whipped cream for garnish
Ground cinnamon or raspberries for garnish

Pour the cream and milk into a saucepan, and scald over medium heat. Remove from the heat and stir in sugar and coffee granules until dissolved. Mix in vanilla extract. In a mixing bowl, beat yolks until thick and creamy. Stir the hot cream mixture into the yolks and then pour the egg-cream mixture into a 1-quart baking dish. Set the dish in a pan with hot water to reach 1 inch up the sides of the dish and bake in a preheated 325° F. oven for 30 to 35 minutes, or until set. Remove from the oven and let cool. Refrigerate for at least 2 hours. Prepare the Chocolate Cups.

Spoon the chilled custard into Chocolate Cups, leaving a small indentation in the center of the coffee cream. Into each indentation pour 2 teaspoons coffee liqueur. Top with whipped cream and sprinkle with cinnamon or decorate with raspberries. Makes 6 servings.

Jordan

ESTATE BOTTLED
1982
Cabernet Sauvignon
Alexander Valley

GROWN, PRODUCED & BOTTLED BY JORDAN VINEYARD & WINERY
ALEXANDER VALLEY, HEALDSBURG, CA. BW 4776 • ALCOHOL 12.8% BY VOLUME

JORDAN WINERY

No roadside marker identifies the sinuous road that leads to Jordan Winery, a spectacular French château set on an oak-studded hilltop in the Alexander Valley. Owned by Tom and Sally Jordan, the ocher winery and secluded manor-style home are headquarters of one of America's finest wine-making ventures.

Here is the fruition of a young family's dream. Formerly city dwellers from Denver, the Jordans are now solidly ensconced in a life of country gentility. An aura of mystique surrounds their life style.

Though united in interest and goals, they are a couple with opposite facets in their personalities. Chicly garbed in designer outfits, Sally sparkles with ricocheting humor and gracious warmth. Her skill as a hostess is peerless, and she is able to put her guests instantly at ease.

Soft-spoken Tom is a thinker, a businessman, and a scientist. Likely attired in cowboy boots and chinos, he operates the Jordan Oil and Gas Company, based in Santa Rosa, in tandem with the winery.

The Jordans are natives of Illinois. In her youth Sally was a rally girl at Stanford University and a 1956 graduate in English literature. They met when she was teaching at Colorado Women's College in Denver and Tom was attending law school nearby.

Married for over twenty five years, wine has always been part of the Jordans' life style and owning a winery their dream. Their early goal was to purchase a French château; then they discovered California wine. The win-

ery and vineyards were founded in 1972, on 280 acres.

Characteristically choosing his own path, Tom set out to make a wine to please his own palate. "I love the Bordeaux style," he explains. The result is elegant, drinkable wines the day they are released.

Sally's role includes entertaining a parade of international dignitaries and visitors at their showplace estate and running the family home, where she is the cook. The winery has its own chef for guest functions.

A lover of animals, she cares for a menagerie: peacocks, llamas, turtles, German shepherds, and assorted wild ducks and geese. She also oversees vegetable and flower gardens.

The winery facility has one wing designed solely for entertaining, complete with three bedroom suites that overlook both the barrel rooms and vineyards. Each suite is decorated with a different period of French furnishings. Crystal chandeliers illuminate the dining room, which seats twenty four, and the adjacent contemporary kitchen, done in blue-and-white Portuguese tile, contains the latest appliances.

"Physically we orchestrate the table to feature the wine," she says. The picture-perfect table is set with hand-embroidered Madeira linens, fine crystal, and eye-catching bouquets. Grape-gathering baskets bearing greenery adorn the walls.

The Jordan culinary style is California-French with European service. "We believe the integrity of the ingredient must be maintained, just as the integrity of the variety must be pure in the wine," explains Sally. "The joys of the table have always been our hobby. In the early years of our marriage Tom and I loved his wine cellar and my cooking.

"The winery was our dream," continues Sally. "Yet we are an outspoken family and the chefs here must have distinctive, fascinating ingredients that are wonderfully fresh. The chefs have to be innovators, explorers. They must keep us amused. After all, if it isn't fun, we'll raise rutabagas instead."

Raw Beef Salad with Ginger and Soy Sauce

1 large filet mignon (about ¾ pound)
Ginger and Soy Sauce (recipe follows)
Red-leaf lettuce
1 cucumber
1 small bunch enoki mushrooms for garnish
Cilantro sprigs for garnish

Trim fillet of any fat. Wrap it in plastic wrap and place in the freezer for 1 hour to firm up so as to facilitate slicing. Prepare the Ginger and Soy Sauce.

Cut the beef into ¼-inch-thick slices, allowing 3 slices per person. Place the slices between 2 sheets of waxed paper and pound to ⅛-inch thickness with a meat mallet. Place 1 or 2 lettuce leaves on each plate. Overlap 3 slices of beef on each lettuce bed. Drizzle Ginger and Soy Sauce over the beef. Peel the cucumber and slice thinly. Arrange slices in a fan next to the beef. Garnish with enoki mushrooms, if desired, and top with a sprig of cilantro. Makes 6 servings.

Ginger and Soy Sauce Place in a blender ¼ cup soy sauce, 2 tablespoons Oriental-style sesame oil, 1½ teaspoons bottled Chinese black beans with chili sauce (optional), 1 egg yolk, 1½ teaspoons granulated sugar, 1 tablespoon rice wine or sake, 1½ teaspoons rice-wine vinegar, and 2 tablespoons minced fresh ginger root. Blend until smooth. Chill 1 hour.

Grilled Salmon Fillets with Chili Hollandaise

1 tablespoon each fresh lemon juice and water
¼ teaspoon salt
2 egg yolks
12 tablespoons (¾ cup) unsalted butter, melted and kept warm
½ cup fresh corn kernels
½ cup peeled and diced prickly pear (¼-inch dice)
1½ tablespoons chopped fresh cilantro
Pinch ground cayenne pepper
½ teaspon chili powder
1 teaspoon tomato paste
6 salmon fillets (about 5 ounces each)

In a blender or a food processor fitted with a metal blade, combine the lemon juice, water, salt, and egg yolks. Blend for a few seconds and transfer to a bowl. Gradually pour in the warm melted butter, whisking constantly. Blanch corn kernels in boiling salted water for 2 minutes and drain. Blanch prickly pear in boiling salted water for 3 minutes and drain. Add the corn kernels, prickly pear, cilantro, cayenne, chili powder, and tomato paste to the sauce and mix well.

Meanwhile, grill salmon fillets over a medium-hot fire, turning once, until slightly underdone or fish just barely flakes with a fork, about 5 minutes. Spoon a pool of warm sauce onto each serving plate. Place a salmon fillet in the center of the plate and spoon a thin strip of sauce across the salmon. Makes 6 servings.

Chardonnay Sorbet with Berries

Sugar Syrup (recipe follows)
1 cup Chardonnay
1 cup white grape juice (Chardonnay, if available, or Chenin Blanc)
½ teaspoon fresh lemon juice
Fresh grape leaves
Blueberries, raspberries, and strawberries or *fraises des bois* (wild strawberries)

Prepare the Sugar Syrup. Pour the Chardonnay into a saucepan, heat to boiling, remove from the heat, and cool to room temperature. Stir in the grape juice, Sugar Syrup, and lemon juice. Freeze mixture in an ice-cream freezer following manufacturer's instructions. For each serving, arrange scoops of the sorbet on a grape leaf and surround with a variety of fresh berries. Makes 6 servings, or about 1½ quarts.

Sugar Syrup Place in a saucepan 1½ cups water and ¾ cup granulated sugar. Stir over low heat until sugar dissolves and the syrup is completely clear.

MENU

Recipes by Jordan Winery Chef Franco Dunn

PRAWNS WITH SAFFRON SAUCE*
JORDAN WINERY CHARDONNAY

•

**MEDALLIONS OF VENISON
WITH CRANBERRIES***
WILD RICE WITH MUSHROOMS
BRAISED FENNEL
JORDAN WINERY
CABERNET SAUVIGNON

•

**WHITE CHOCOLATE MOUSSE WITH
FOUR TREASURES***

Prawns with Saffron Sauce

16 medium-size prawns
5 tablespoons unsalted butter
1 shallot, finely chopped
¼ cup Cognac or Grand Marnier
½ cup Chardonnay or other dry white wine
1 cup whipping cream (not ultra-pasteurized)
2 pinches powdered saffron
Dash Tabasco sauce

Peel and devein prawns, reserving shells. In a saucepan, melt 2 tablespoons butter and sauté prawn shells and shallots until shells turn pink and shallots are limp. Pour Cognac over the shells and shallots and ignite with a match. When flames die, add wine and reduce over medium heat to 3 tablespoons. Strain, discard shells, and return liquid to saucepan. Add cream, saffron, and Tabasco and reduce over medium-high heat until sauce coats the back of a spoon, about 10 minutes. Whisk in 2 tablespoons butter. Keep warm.

In a skillet, melt remaining 1 tablespoon butter and sauté prawns until they curl slightly, about 3 minutes. Spoon a pool of sauce onto each serving plate. Place prawns on sauce and serve at once. Makes 4 servings.

Medallions of Venison with Cranberries

2 cups water
2 cups fresh cranberries
¼ cup granulated sugar
Peel of 1 orange (without any white membrane), finely chopped
1 2-inch cinnamon stick
Pinch ground cayenne pepper
4 venison medallions, cut from the loin (about 5 ounces each)
8 tablespoons (¼ pound or ½ cup) unsalted butter
1½ tablespoons finely chopped shallots
½ cup Cabernet Sauvignon or other dry red wine
1 cup veal or chicken stock
Salt and freshly ground black pepper to taste

In a saucepan, combine the water, cranberries, sugar, orange peel, cinnamon, and cayenne. Bring to a boil, lower the heat slightly, and simmer until cranberry skins pop. Drain, remove cinnamon stick, and set cranberries aside.

In a skillet, sauté venison medallions in 2 tablespoons butter, turning to brown both sides and cooking until rare. Transfer to a platter and keep warm in a 200° F. oven. Add shallots to the pan drippings and sauté until soft. Deglaze pan with wine and stock and cook over high heat to reduce to ½ cup. Lower the heat to medium and whisk in remaining 6 tablespoons butter, bit by bit. Add cranberries and heat through. Place medallions on individual plates and spoon sauce over them. Makes 4 servings.

White Chocolate Mousse with Four Treasures

4 ounces white chocolate chips
¼ pound (½ cup) unsalted butter
2 eggs, separated and at room temperature
2½ tablespoons granulated sugar

Four Treasures

¼ cup roasted skinned hazelnuts
8 strawberries
Mixture of 1½ teaspoons each granulated sugar and dark rum
Peel of 1 orange (without any white membrane), cut into matchstick
¼ cup each water and granulated sugar
4 Italian amaretto cookies

Melt chocolate in the top pan of a double boiler placed over simmering water. In a separate pan, melt the butter. Combine the melted chocolate and butter in a mixing bowl and whisk until blended. Add egg yolks, one at a time, and continue whisking about 5 minutes, or until the mixture is creamy and thick. In a separate bowl, beat the egg whites until soft peaks form. Gradually add sugar and continue to beat until stiff peaks form. Stir one-half the egg whites into the chocolate mixture to lighten it, then gently fold in the remaining egg whites. Spoon into small dessert bowls. Cover and chill overnight.

Shortly before serving, prepare the Four Treasures. Coarsely chop the hazelnuts. Cut strawberries into sixths and marinate in the sugar-rum mixture. Combine the orange peel, water, and 3 tablespoons sugar in a saucepan and cook at a slow simmer, adding more water as needed, until peel is tender and soft, about 10 minutes. Drain off simmering liquid and arrange peel on a wire rack to dry. When dry, toss with remaining 1 tablespoon sugar. Coarsely chop the cookies.

To serve, unmold each mousse (it may be necessary to loosen edges with a knife) and place in the center of a dessert plate. Frame each mousse with little piles of the "treasures." Makes 4 servings.

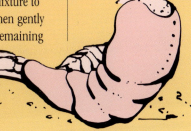

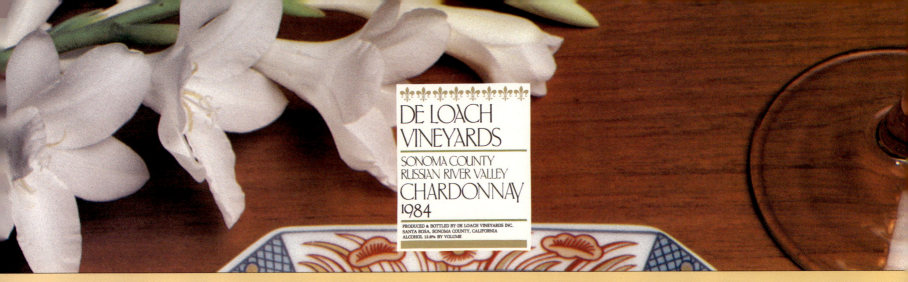

DE LOACH
VINEYARDS

SONOMA COUNTY
RUSSIAN RIVER VALLEY
CHARDONNAY
1984

PRODUCED & BOTTLED BY DE LOACH VINEYARDS INC.
SANTA ROSA, SONOMA COUNTY, CALIFORNIA
ALCOHOL 13.0% BY VOLUME

DE LOACH VINEYARDS

Vintner Cecil De Loach was once a San Francisco fireman with a burning desire to be a farmer. In 1969 he realized his dream. He staked his claim on an old Zinfandel vineyard on Olivet Road in Santa Rosa and settled down to grow grapes and fruit trees between shifts at the firehouse.

With his wife, Christine, and sons John and Michael, he built a home on the ranch and moved to the country in the early seventies. Cecil became interested in wine and wine making and took extension courses in oenology and wine chemistry from the University of California, Davis. By 1975 he felt ready to begin making wine professionally.

In 1979 Cecil built, with his own hands, a 3,200-square-foot mission-style winery. For ten years he had been commuting to fight fires to augment his earnings from the fruit crops. In 1980 he resigned from the San Francisco Fire Department, where he had served for sixteen years, to devote full-time to his winery and vineyards.

The family completed an addition to the winery in 1984, tripling the original building's size. Construction of the new facility, like everything else done by the De Loaches, was a family affair. Cecil served as designer and general ramrod of the project.

"We've always done everything with money generated internally," Cecil explains, "as there is no family fortune or stock portfolio to finance my winery."

The family radiates enthusiasm for the rural life style. They are all involved in the winery, including Michael's wife Rachel, and they all love to cook.

Most of Christine's entertaining is

impromptu—a late brunch with houseguests or lunch or dinner. The De Loaches' hospitality is informal. They let guests come into the kitchen as they prepare a meal or put the finishing touches on a dish.

Cecil is an accomplished chef, a talent he perfected during years of cooking for hungry firemen. He is the pro at breakfast. The sons are also fine cooks. "Because the boys saw their dad cook as they were growing up, they became involved in the kitchen," explains Christine.

The farm's garden and orchard provide year-round produce. "Tomatoes we can't do without," says Christine. "We have lots of herbs and use their blossoms as well. We have a ton of wild blackberries and raspberries, loganberries, pears, apples, and peaches."

In his spare time, Cecil enjoys flying, fishing, and horseback riding. His background is much more complex than the years as a fireman reveal. His childhood was spent in Macon, Georgia, where his grandfather was a Baptist missionary. The family moved to San Francisco when he was seven and following high school he enlisted in the Marine Corps. He graduated from San Francisco State University with honors in physical anthropology and then did research in urban anthropology at San Francisco's Langley-Porter Clinic, under a grant from the National Institute of Mental Health.

Christine is a third-generation Californian who also majored in anthropology at San Francisco State. Of Scottish, English, and Irish heritage, she is a trim, vibrant woman with deep-blue eyes.

Operating 150 acres of vineyards and turning out well-crafted award-winning wines keep the De Loach family on the run.

MENU

PROSCIUTTO AND BLACK FIGS
DE LOACH VINEYARDS
WHITE ZINFANDEL

•

OSSO BUCO*
RISOTTO ALLA MILANESE*
GREEN BEAN BUNDLES
STEAMED SUMMER SQUASH WITH
RED BELL PEPPER STRIPS
DE LOACH VINEYARDS PINOT NOIR
DE LOACH VINEYARDS
CABERNET SAUVIGNON

•

CARAMEL CUSTARD*
DE LOACH VINEYARDS
LATE HARVEST GEWÜRZTRAMINER

Osso Buco
8 2-inch-thick slices
   veal shank (4 to 5
   pounds)
Flour seasoned with
   salt and freshly
   ground black
   pepper
2 tablespoons butter
1½ cups Fumé Blanc
   or other dry white
   wine
1 pound Italian plum
   tomatoes, peeled
   and diced
1½ cups veal or
   chicken stock
½ teaspoon salt
¼ teaspoon freshly
   ground black
   pepper
2 cloves garlic, finely
   chopped
2 teaspoons grated
   lemon peel
¼ cup chopped fresh
   parsley

In a large bowl, dredge the shanks with the seasoned flour. In a heavy 12-inch skillet, melt the butter over medium heat. Add the shank pieces and sauté 5 to 6 minutes, or until they are nicely browned on all sides. Transfer shanks to a large flameproof pot. Place the pot over low heat, add the wine, and simmer 5 minutes. Stir in the tomatoes, stock, salt, and pepper. Cover the pot and place in a preheated 325° F. oven for 1½ hours, or until meat is tender. Remove shanks to a serving dish and pour sauce into a pitcher. Mix together garlic, lemon peel, and parsley and scatter over the meat. Pass the sauce. Makes 8 servings.

Risotto alla Milanese
6 tablespoons butter
½ pound fresh
   mushrooms, sliced
4½ cups chicken stock
1 small onion, minced
2 cups long-grain
   white rice or
   Arborio rice (see
   Note)
½ cup Fumé Blanc or
   other dry white
   wine
⅛ teaspoon saffron
   threads
½ cup freshly grated
   Parmesan cheese

In a skillet placed over medium heat, melt 2 tablespoons butter, add mushrooms, and sauté for 5 minutes; remove from the heat and set aside. Pour the stock into a saucepan and bring to a simmer. In a 3-quart flameproof casserole, melt 2 tablespoons butter and sauté onion over medium heat, stirring, for 8 to 10 minutes until golden. Add rice and sauté, stirring, for 2 minutes, until rice is well coated and has an opalescent appearance. Add wine and cook, uncovered, over medium heat until wine is nearly absorbed. Add 2 cups hot stock and cook, uncovered, stirring occasionally, until liquid is almost absorbed. Add 1 more cup hot stock and repeat.

Meanwhile, add the saffron to remaining 1½ cups stock and steep a few minutes. Pour this over rice and cook, stirring occasionally, until stock is absorbed and rice is tender. Reduce the heat to low. With a fork, stir in the sautéed mushrooms, the remaining 2 tablespoons butter, and the grated cheese. Heat gently and serve. Makes 8 servings.

Note *Arborio rice is a short-grained rice from northern Italy. It can be purchased at specialty food markets and some supermarkets.*

Caramel Custard
1 cup granulated sugar
3½ cups milk, or 1¾
   cups each whipping
   cream and milk
6 eggs
Pinch salt
1 teaspoon vanilla
   extract
¼ teaspoon freshly
   grated nutmeg
Toasted slivered
   almonds for garnish

Heat ½ cup of the sugar in a heavy saucepan until it melts and

caramelizes, shaking pan frequently. All at once, pour caramelized sugar into a 1½-quart ring mold or baking dish, then tilt the mold to coat bottom and sides evenly with caramelized sugar; set mold aside.

In the saucepan used to make the caramel, scald the milk over medium heat. Beat eggs until light and beat in remaining ½ cup sugar. Stir in scalded milk, salt, vanilla, and nutmeg. Pour egg mixture into caramel-coated mold. Place mold in a pan with hot water to reach about 1 inch up the sides of the mold. Bake in a preheated 325° F. oven for 35 minutes, or until set. Remove mold from hot water and cool on a rack at least 1 hour. To unmold, dip mold quickly almost to rim in hot water to loosen caramel, then invert onto a serving plate. Sprinkle the top of the mold with toasted almonds. Makes 8 servings.

MENU
FRESH FRUIT SALAD
FIREHOUSE FRITTATA*
STEAMED WHOLE ARTICHOKES
SOURDOUGH FRENCH BREAD
DE LOACH VINEYARDS
WHITE ZINFANDEL
•
GRANDMA D'S POUND CAKE*
DE LOACH VINEYARDS
LATE HARVEST GEWÜRZTRAMINER

Firehouse Frittata
- 1 pound mild Italian sausages
- 1 medium-size onion, chopped
- 12 eggs
- 1 cup fresh button mushrooms (about ¼ pound)
- 2 to 3 medium-size zucchini, thinly sliced
- ¼ pound Monterey Jack cheese, thinly sliced
- 6 tomato slices (3⁄8 inch thick)
- Salt and freshly ground black pepper to taste
- 2 teaspoons chopped fresh oregano, or ½ teaspoon dried oregano, crumbled
- Dry fine sourdough French bread crumbs
- Freshly grated Parmesan cheese

Remove casing from sausages and break up meat into a 10-inch ovenproof skillet. Add onion to skillet and sauté over medium heat until meat and onion are fully cooked; remove from the heat. Beat eggs until light and pour over meat. Scatter whole mushrooms and zucchini over egg and top first with a layer of Jack cheese, and then with a layer of tomato slices. Sprinkle with salt, and pepper, and oregano. Dust liberally with bread crumbs and Parmesan cheese. Bake frittata in a preheated 350° F. oven for 35 to 40 minutes, or until set and lightly browned on top. Remove from the oven and let stand 10 minutes. Cut into wedges to serve. Makes 6 to 8 servings.

Grandma D's Pound Cake
- ½ pound (1 cup) butter
- 3 cups granulated sugar
- 6 eggs
- 3 cups cake flour
- 1 cup whipping cream
- 1 tablespoon vanilla extract
- 1 teaspoon lemon extract

Have all ingredients at room temperature. In a mixing bowl, cream butter and sugar until light and fluffy. Add eggs, one at a time, stirring until well combined. Alternating between the two, gradually mix in flour and cream until thoroughly blended. Stir in vanilla and lemon extracts. Spoon into a greased and floured 10-inch tube pan. Bake in a preheated 350° F. oven for 1 hour, or until a toothpick inserted in center comes out clean. Let cool on a rack before removing from pan. Makes 16 servings.

Heitz Cellar
1981
NAPA VALLEY
CABERNET SAUVIGNON
ALCOHOL 13½% BY VOLUME
PRODUCED AND BOTTLED IN OUR CELLAR BY
HEITZ WINE CELLARS
ST. HELENA, CALIFORNIA, U.S.A.

HEITZ CELLARS

Heitz Cellars is in the fullest sense a family winery. Joe Heitz, the president and wine maker, considers his involvement with wine a matter of fate. During the Second World War, the Illinois-born Heitz moonlighted as a cellarman at a San Joaquin Valley winery between shifts as a ground crewman for a fighter squadron.

He quickly recognized his palate for wine and, at war's end, enrolled as a student of oenology at the University of California, Davis. Following graduation he worked throughout the state as a wine maker for established firms and as a teacher of winemaking at Fresno State College.

In 1961 he and his wife, Alice, began the winery on St. Helena Highway South, in the tiny building that now serves as salesroom. In 1964 the family bought its present home ranch in Spring Valley, a narrow fold in the hills just east of St. Helena. The secluded property wears an air of well-being; it is the sort of place birds come to sing on a spring morning.

The land was developed as a vineyard and winery in the 1880s by Anton Rossi. Records show he made about ten thousand gallons of wine yearly in the fine old stone building that now holds Heitz white wines. A second structure, built in 1972, handles the red wines, first in stainless-steel fermenters, then in a complex variety of oak tanks and barrels made from American and European forests.

Heitz Cellars has achieved much of its reputation for greatness from its Martha's Vineyard Cabernet Sauvignon. These grapes come from the vineyards of Tom and Martha May, set on a gravelly bench in the western foothills of the valley near Oakville. This Cabernet is the standard by which wine critics often judge other California Cabernets. The family's reserve/release policy means that as many as five vintages of this wine are available at one time, along with as many other more modest, and more reasonably priced Cabernets. The winery's total annual production numbers around forty thousand cases.

Alice, who also hails from the Midwest, earned a business degree in college. As vice-president, she manages customer relations—sometimes from the tasting room, but more often as the creator of memorable meals to set off the wines. Her preference is sit-down dinners for eight or more, clustered around the big round table in the dining room of their two-story woodframe house. This way the Heitzes can pour a wide selection of wines.

Their two sons and daughter are involved in the family wine business. "The boys are wonderful cooks, besides," exclaims Alice. David serves as wine maker, responsible for the daily operation of the winery. He trained at the University of California, Davis and Fresno State College. Kathleen Heitz Ryan is involved in marketing, having previously taught high-school biology following studies at the American College in Switzerland and the University of Oregon in Eugene. Rollie received a degree in finance from the University of Santa Clara. All three have had long experience in vineyard and cellar work dating back to grammar school days. Alice often turns the entertaining chores over to Rollie as "he loves to barbecue and he bakes anything from scratch." Two grandsons add to the family repertoire.

MENU

BAY SCALLOPS IN WHITE WINE*
HEITZ CHARDONNAY

•

PORK AND RED CABBAGE GRIGNOLINO*
BUTTERED NEW POTATOES
HEITZ GRIGNOLINO

•

APPLES AND BLUE CHEESE
HEITZ TAWNY PORT

Bay Scallops in White Wine

5 tablespoons butter
1 clove garlic, minced
1 cup Chardonnay or other dry white wine
½ teaspoon dried tarragon, crumbled
Salt and freshly ground black pepper to taste
2 pounds bay scallops
2 cups whipping cream
Watercress sprigs for garnish

In a large skillet placed over medium heat, melt 1 tablespoon butter, add garlic, and sauté 1 minute. Add wine and tarragon and simmer until reduced to ½ cup. Add salt, pepper, and scallops and simmer gently until cooked, about 2 to 3 minutes. Remove scallops with a slotted spoon. Keep warm.

Increase heat and reduce juices in skillet to a glaze. Add cream and simmer until sauce thickens, about 15 minutes. Add remaining 4 tablespoons butter and whisk to blend in well. Spoon a shallow pool of sauce onto each serving plate, arrange scallops over sauce, and garnish with watercress. Makes 8 servings.

Pork and Red Cabbage Grignolino

1 boneless pork roast (about 4 pounds)
3 tablespoons butter
2 carrots, thinly sliced
2 onions, sliced
1 large red cabbage, cut into ½-inch-wide strips
2 tart apples, peeled, cored, and cut into ½-inch dice
3 cloves garlic, minced
1 bay leaf
⅛ teaspoon each ground cloves and freshly grated nutmeg
Salt to taste
⅛ teaspoon freshly ground black pepper
3 cups Grignolino
2½ cups rich beef stock

In a skillet, sear surface of pork roast, browning it well on all sides. Meanwhile, melt butter in a large dutch oven, add carrots and onions, and sauté for 10 to 12 minutes, cooking until glazed. Add cabbage and sauté until well coated with the butter and vegetable juices, about 5 minutes. Add apples, garlic, bay leaf, cloves, nutmeg, salt, pepper, Grignolino, and stock. Bring to a boil, reduce the heat to a simmer, and add pork.

Cover and simmer gently for 2 hours, or until pork is tender. To serve, slice meat, arrange on a platter, and serve vegetables in a separate bowl. Makes 8 to 10 servings.

MENU

NAPA CABBAGE AND SHRIMP SALAD*
HEITZ CHARDONNAY

•

BREASTS OF CHICKEN OPORTO*
BROCCOLI WITH LEMON BUTTER*
HEITZ CHARDONNAY

•

RASPBERRY ICE
ALMOND COOKIES

Napa Cabbage and Shrimp Salad

1 small Napa cabbage (about 1½ pounds)
½ pound small cooked shrimp
1 red bell pepper, seeded and cut in julienne
Mustard and Tarragon Vinaigrette (recipe follows)
2 tablespoons chopped fresh cilantro

Cut cabbage into 1-inch-wide pieces and place in a bowl with shrimp and bell pepper. Mix lightly. Prepare the Mustard and Tarragon Vinaigrette and pour over salad. Toss gently. Sprinkle with cilantro. Makes 6 servings.

Mustard and Tarragon Vinaigrette

In a jar with a tight-fitting lid, combine 2 teaspoons Dijon-style mustard, ½ teaspoon dried tarragon, crumbled, ¼ teaspoon freshly ground black pepper, ⅓ cup olive oil, and 2 tablespoons white-wine vinegar. Twist lid onto jar and shake well.

Breasts of Chicken Oporto

3 tablespoons butter
6 boned chicken breast halves
2 teaspoons chopped fresh tarragon, or ½ teaspoon dried tarragon, crumbled
6 small white onions, thinly sliced
½ cup Port
3 tablespoons dry Sherry
½ cup rich chicken stock (see Note)
Salt and freshly ground black pepper to taste
Dash freshly grated nutmeg
1 cup sour cream

In a skillet, melt 1 tablespoon butter and sauté chicken breasts lightly until browned; remove from pan and keep warm. Immerse fresh tarragon in boiling water for 5 seconds; drain. (Omit this step if dried tarragon is used.) Pound tarragon to a paste with the remaining 2 tablespoons butter.

Melt flavored butter in the same skillet used for browning the chicken. Add onions and sauté, stirring constantly until onions are delicately colored. Stir in wines and stock and simmer for 5 minutes. Place chicken breasts in sauce, cover, and simmer gently 5 to 10 minutes, or until cooked through. Season with salt, pepper, and nutmeg. Stir in sour cream and heat just until blended. Makes 6 servings. ***Note:*** *To achieve a rich stock for this dish, boil 2 cups regular-strength chicken stock until reduced to ½ cup.*

Broccoli With Lemon Butter

1 large bunch broccoli
3 tablespoons butter
2 teaspoons fresh lemon juice
3 tablespoons chopped walnuts

Cut broccoli into long, thin strips and steam until tender, about 7 minutes. Remove from steamer and arrange on serving dish. Meanwhile, melt butter and add lemon juice and walnuts. Spoon hot butter sauce over steamed broccoli. Makes 6 servings.

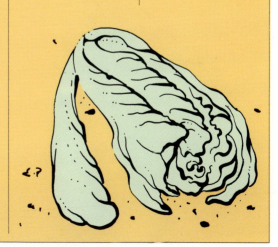

CALIFORNIA
CHAMPAGNE

Hanns·Kornell

BRUT

ALCOHOL 12% BY VOL.   750 ML 125.4 FL OZ.)

PRODUCED AND BOTTLED BY
HANNS KORNELL CHAMPAGNE CELLARS
ST. HELENA, NAPA VALLEY, CALIFORNIA

NATURALLY FERMENTED IN THIS BOTTLE // METHODE CHAMPENOISE

HANNS KORNELL
CHAMPAGNE CELLARS

In 1940 Hanns Kornell fled Nazi-controlled Germany, and not long after arrived almost penniless in the United States. From the beginning he was determined to continue the family tradition of producing fine Champagnes, as his ancestors had done in the Rhineland since 1780. Notable among his relatives was an uncle, Eugene Schoenberger, who had run one of Germany's largest Champagne cellars, Schoenberger Kabinet.

Hanns's first goal, however, was survival, which he managed by washing dishes and doing other jobs, until California, with its promise of opportunity, beckoned.

Hitchhiking across the country with only two dollars in his pocket, Hanns finally reached California and immediately began plying his trade as Champagne master. From there he returned east and made Champagne for the Gibson Wine Company in Cincinnati and Kentucky, and later moved to St. Louis to oversee Cook's Imperial Champagne for the American Wine Company.

By 1952 he had saved enough money to make a small start on his own. He borrowed three thousand dollars from a friend, drove his convertible to California, and rented an old winery in Sonoma. While waiting for his Champagnes to mature and age, Hanns sold wine in San Francisco from a battered old truck by day, and continued to produce new Champagnes by night.

In 1958 he found his ideal location, the historic stone Larkmead Cellars, built in 1864 just north of St. Helena. He moved to Napa Valley with his bride, Marilouise, a talented Californian of Italian-Swiss parentage.

Her disciplines were education, medicine, and music. She had pursued medical studies at the University of California and founded the first cerebral palsy school in the Bay Area. She also studied voice, making her concert debut in San Francisco. Today their children, Paul and Peter are actively engaged in marketing, public relations, and production at the winery.

When the Kornells entertain, Marilouise plans the menu around what is fresh in the garden: vegetables, berries, and orchard fruits. She enjoys intimate dinners for six or eight and also does brunches, "as they are ideal with Champagne."

Hanns produces approximately sixty thousand cases of *méthode champenoise* from wine that he purchases. Blending the wines for the various styles of Champagne is a family affair, as his is a low-key, hand-crafted operation.

He feels strongly that it is an advantage to be able to choose the base for his Champagnes from among finished wines. Hanns also clashes with purists by choosing the Johannisberg Riesling grape for his finest Champagne, rather than the Chardonnay and Pinot Noir grapes of classic French bottlings.

To compose the blend, Hanns first brings about ten bottles of bulk-wine samples into the office, where he and his staff taste them under various conditions for a couple weeks. The best of these he then takes home for the final test with his family. The wines are blended and tasted in the kitchen "before my wife starts cooking," says Hanns, because cooking odors destroy the sensitivity of the palate.

When they finally agree, the wine is bought—some two hundred thousand or three hundred thousand gallons of it from three or four wineries. Sometimes that isn't the end of it. One year he had to send back one hundred thousand gallons because the wine that was delivered wasn't the same as the sample.

MENU

CARROT AND GINGER SOUP*
HANNS KORNELL BRUT CHAMPAGNE

•

TRUFFLED CAPON*
SAUTÉED SNOW PEAS,
CARROTS, AND FENNEL
OVEN-ROASTED POTATOES
BELGIAN ENDIVE SALAD WITH CHÈVRE*
HANNS KORNELL BLANC DE BLANCS

•

GOBLETS OF STRAWBERRIES
IN CHAMPAGNE
HANNS KORNELL MUSCAT ALEXANDRIA

Carrot and Ginger Soup

2 tablespoons unsalted butter
1 large onion, chopped
¼ cup finely chopped fresh ginger root
3 cloves garlic, minced
⅛ teaspoon curry powder
7 cups chicken stock
2 cups Brut Champagne or other dry white wine
1½ pounds carrots, peeled and cut into ½-inch pieces
2 tablespoons fresh lemon juice
Salt and freshly ground black pepper to taste
Snipped fresh chives or chopped fresh parsley for garnish

Melt the butter in a large stockpot placed over medium heat. Add the onion, ginger, garlic, and curry powder and sauté for 5 minutes. Add the stock, wine, and carrots and bring to a boil. Reduce the heat to medium and simmer uncovered until the carrots are very tender, about 45 minutes. Season with lemon juice, salt, and pepper.

Cool the soup slightly, then purée in a blender or a food processor fitted with a metal blade. Serve hot or chilled, sprinkled with chives. Makes 6 servings.

Truffled Capon

1 can (½ ounce) whole truffle
Salt and freshly ground black pepper to taste
Brandy
1 capon (about 10 pounds)
1½ pounds bulk country sausage
⅓ cup each brandy and dry Sherry
2 eggs, beaten
Unsalted butter
½ pound fresh mushrooms (about 1 inch in diameter)
2 tablespoons butter

Remove the truffle from the can; reserve the can liquid. Thinly slice the truffle, making 10 slices in all. Sprinkle the slices with salt, pepper, and brandy. Loosen the skin from the breast of the capon by slipping your fingers between the skin and the flesh of the fowl, working from the body cavity opening. Lay 4 truffle slices in a neat pattern over each breast, being careful not to break the skin. Now, loosen the skin from the legs and insert 1 truffle slice between the meat and the skin of each leg. Wrap the capon in plastic wrap and refrigerate overnight to allow the truffle flavor to permeate the bird.

The next day, mix together the sausage, ⅓ cup each brandy and Sherry, eggs, and reserved truffle juice. Stuff the neck and body cavities with the sausage mixture. Sew the vent closed and truss the bird. Rub the surface of the bird with unsalted butter. Lay it on its side in a deep roasting pan and place in a preheated 400° F. oven for 15 minutes. Turn bird to the other side and roast

for 15 minutes; now turn again and roast for another 15 minutes. Lower the oven heat to 375° F. and roast for 1½ hours, or until tender, turning the bird every 15 minutes. Transfer the capon to a heated platter.

Remove the stems from the mushrooms and sauté caps in 2 tablespoons butter until tender, about 5 to 7 minutes. Garnish the platter with the mushroom caps. Makes 8 to 10 servings.

Belgian Endive Salad with Chèvre

Walnut Oil Vinaigrette (recipe follows)
6 or 7 large heads Belgian endive
3 tablespoons coarsely ground walnuts
Freshly ground black pepper to taste
6 ounces California chèvre
1 red Delicious apple

Prepare the Walnut Oil Vinaigrette. Trim and core the endives and cut leaves into julienne. Place in a chilled bowl along with the walnuts. Pour vinaigrette over greens and toss well. Spoon greens onto individual salad plates and grind pepper over the top. Center each plate of greens with a portion of the chèvre. Core and thinly slice the apple. Arrange the apple slices in a spoke fashion, radiating from the chèvre. Makes 6 servings.

Walnut Oil Vinaigrette In a jar with a tight-fitting lid, combine ½ teaspoon salt, ¼ teaspoon freshly ground black pepper, 2 tablespoons white-wine vinegar, and 6 tablespoons walnut oil. Twist lid onto jar and shake well.

MENU

SMOKED SALMON
HANNS KORNELL BRUT IN MAGNUMS

•

ROAST LOIN OF VEAL
WITH HAZELNUTS*
FETTUCCINE WITH PESTO SAUCE*
CARROT SLICES WITH LEMON BUTTER
WATERCRESS SALAD
HANNS KORNELL BLANC DE BLANCS

•

NECTARINES WITH RASPBERRY PURÉE*
HANNS KORNELL MUSCAT ALEXANDRIA

Roast Loin of Veal with Hazelnuts

1 veal loin (3 to 4 pounds, after trimming)
½ cup seasoned dry bread crumbs
1 cup chopped hazelnuts
¼ pound (½ cup) butter, melted
1 tablespoon Dijon-style mustard

Ask your butcher to trim and clean the veal loin, including the fell, or silvery membrane. Mix together the bread crumbs, nuts, butter, and mustard and pat the mixture on the top and sides of the loin.

Place the meat on a rack in a roasting pan and insert a meat thermometer into the thickest portion. Roast in a preheated 350° F. oven for about 40 minutes, or until the thermometer registers 125° F. Remove the loin from the oven and let rest 15 minutes before slicing. Makes 8 servings.

Fettucine with Pesto Sauce

Pesto Sauce (recipe follows)
1½ pounds fresh fettucine
½ cup freshly grated Parmesan cheese

Prepare the Pesto Sauce. Cook fettucine in a large pot of boiling salted water until al dente, about 3 minutes; drain. Turn out on a hot platter and mix with the Pesto Sauce. Sprinkle with Parmesan cheese. Makes 8 servings.

Pesto Sauce In a blender or a food processor fitted with a metal blade, combine 1½ cups lightly packed fresh basil leaves, ¼ cup olive oil, 2 cloves garlic, minced, 3 tablespoons roasted pistachios or pine nuts, and ½ cup freshly grated Parmesan or dry Jack cheese. Blend until smooth and thick.

Nectarines with Raspberry Purée

2 packages (10 ounces each) frozen raspberries in light syrup, thawed
8 nectarines
3 tablespoons toasted slivered blanched almonds

Purée raspberries in a blender or a food processor fitted with a metal blade, then press purée through a sieve to remove seeds. Halve and pit nectarines and place two halves in each dessert bowl. Pour raspberry purée over nectarines and sprinkle with almonds. Makes 8 servings.

McDOWELL VALLEY VINEYARDS

Karen and Richard Keehn of McDowell Valley Vineyards are a pair of inventive cooks. In their commercial-size island kitchen with its copper pots hanging at arms' reach, they turn out great feasts for guests visiting from all over the country.

One dinner, a showcase for their Petite Syrah, featured a mixed grill of suckling pig, venison, breasts of smoked mallard, fresh albacore tuna, crowns of lamb, and beef from their own herd. The grilled foods were served with six sauces so guests could mix and match their favorite combinations. Wine jells and salads from garden greens enhanced the entrées.

"Rich is the better cook," claims Karen. "He opens the refrigerator and can cook foods with unique combinations of textures and flavors that work." While in high school, he held a job at Bob's on Broadway in Burlingame, California; there he learned reductions and knife techniques from a fine black chef whose roots were in the South. Karen excels in sauces, appetizers, and desserts, and they compete on soups.

They particularly favor their Kamato Japanese ceramic smoker for turkey, wild fowl, pork, and lamb. They also enjoy making *ballotines, pâtés,* and *roulades,* working together or taking turns boning, prepping, seasoning, or cooking. "And now our various wine sorbets seem to be creating lots of followers," says Karen.

"We pay a great deal of attention to detail. As in wine, we use a minimum of processing in cooking and take fresh organic foods and handle them with finesse," says Rich. "An herb or spice becomes the bridge to handle

and tie the food with a wine. We consider the time of day, the season, the sweetness, and the body of a food, to see if it can complement similar characteristics in the wine."

The couple spend much of their time on the road, as "we try to be an educational resource to our customers and talk about how to use wine as an ingredient in cooking," explains Karen. "We have put so much effort into our wines. It takes years to bring them to the table, so we want them to show well."

The Keehns purchased their historic vineyard in 1970, following their marriage. Karen was a widow and each partner had four children, three girls and a boy. Combined, the children's ages ran in stair steps, a year apart, from age four to twelve.

Neither adult had wine experience in his or her background. Rich had spent fourteen years in the military as an experimental test pilot. Karen, who grew up in Mendocino, California, had a history degree from Stanford University. They wanted a rural life style in which to raise their large family.

Rich and Karen designed and built the winery and their ranch-style home in 1979. They acted as their own general contractor and also did the papering, tiling, and painting themselves. The buildings, located on opposite sides of Highway 175, are surrounded by estate vineyards and pastureland. Pigs are raised in addition to cattle, and vegetable, herb, and flower gardens and orchards augment the table.

"Our style of entertaining and cuisine might be described as rustic elegance or American contemporary. It is an improvisation on whatever is fresh, using wines as an ingredient to reinforce flavors and enhance the resulting food and wine combination," explains Karen. "Food and wine is one way we 'nurture' friends and family."

MENU

MIXED GREENS WITH
WARM BRIE DRESSING*
McDOWELL FUMÉ BLANC

•

BEEF ROLL-UP WITH
MUSHROOM WINE SAUCE*
RED NEW POTATOES WITH
SOUR CREAM AND CAVIAR
WALNUT-ROSEMARY BREAD*
McDOWELL CABERNET SAUVIGNON

•

BAVARIAN BLUE CHEESE WITH APPLES
McDOWELL SYRAH

•

CHERRY CABERNET SORBET
BUTTER COOKIES

Mixed Greens with Warm Brie Dressing

2 tablespoons olive oil
1 shallot, minced
1 clove garlic, minced
⅓ cup Fumé Blanc or other dry white wine
6 ounces Brie cheese
1 teaspoon each chopped fresh parsley and chopped fresh marjoram
3 heads assorted greens, such as butter lettuce, Romaine, curly endive, or red oak-leaf lettuce
2 heads Belgian endive, or 2 avocados

In a skillet, heat oil and sauté shallot and garlic over medium-low heat until transparent, about 5 minutes. Add wine and simmer for 2 to 3 minutes. Break cheese into small pieces and add to the mixture, heating and stirring until the consistency of a creamy salad dressing.

Remove from the heat and stir in parsley and marjoram.

Tear greens into bite-size pieces and place in a salad bowl. Separate endive into individual spears and poke in around edge of bowl, or peel, pit, and dice avocado and add to bowl. Pour warm brie dressing over salad and mix lightly. Makes 8 servings.

Beef Roll-up with Mushroom Wine Sauce

2½ pounds ground lean beef chuck
2 cloves garlic, minced
1 teaspoon salt
¼ teaspoon freshly ground black pepper
1 egg
3 tablespoons minced fresh parsley
2 tablespoons minced fresh marjoram, or 1½ teaspoon dried marjoram, crumbled
½ cup Cabernet Sauvignon or other dry red wine
1 tablespoon rendered bacon fat
⅓ cup each chopped red bell pepper, chopped green bell pepper, shredded carrot, and sliced celery
¼ teaspoon freshly grated nutmeg
½ cup hulled whole pistachios
4 slices bacon
Mushroom Wine Sauce (recipe follows)

In a large bowl, mix together the beef, garlic, salt, pepper, egg, 1½ teaspoons parsley, 1 tablespoon marjoram, and 3 tablespoons wine. In a skillet, melt the bacon fat, add the peppers, carrots, and celery, and sauté until transparent, about 5 minutes; mix in nutmeg and remaining 1 tablespoon marjoram and 1½ tablespoons parsley.

On a sheet of plastic wrap, shape meat mixture into a large patty about ¾ inch thick and 12 inches square. Press nuts evenly into surface of patty. Scatter the sautéed vegetables over the top. Roll up jelly-roll fashion by lifting plastic wrap to help form the roll, and then pinch ends of meat roll together to seal in filling.

Place meat roll in a shallow baking pan. Arrange bacon slices on top of roll to cover as much of it as possible.

Add remaining 5 tablespoons wine to bottom of pan. Bake in a preheated 350° F. oven for 45 to 50 minutes, basting several times with wine, until meat is cooked through but still pink inside. While roll is cooking, prepare the Mushroom Wine Sauce. To serve, ladle pools of Mushroom Wine Sauce onto individual plates. Cut meat roll into 1-inch-thick slices and arrange on sauce. Makes 8 servings.

Mushroom Wine Sauce

In a saucepan, melt 2 tablespoons butter and stir in 2 tablespoons all-purpose flour; cook, stirring, 2 minutes. Whisk in 2 cups hot rich beef stock and ½ Cabernet Sauvignon and simmer until slightly reduced. Season with salt, freshly ground black pepper,

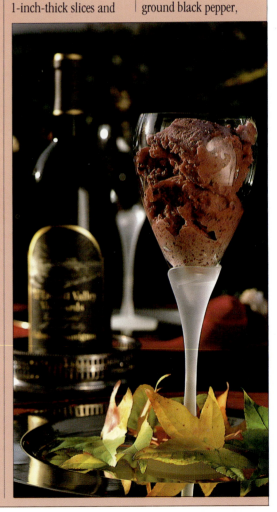

and freshly grated nutmeg to taste. Thinly slice ¾ pound mushrooms. In a skillet, melt 2 tablespoons butter and sauté mushrooms over medium heat until glazed, about 2 minutes. Add to the sauce and heat through.

Walnut-Rosemary Bread

1 package active dry yeast (scant 1 tablespoon)

¼ cup lukewarm water (110° F.)

2½ cups each whole-wheat flour and unbleached flour

2 teaspoons salt

2¼ cups hot water

¼ cup vegetable oil

¼ cup mild-flavored honey

2 tablespoons sesame seeds or wheat germ

⅓ cup chopped walnuts

1 tablespoon minced fresh rosemary

Sprinkle yeast into warm water and let stand until dissolved and foamy, about 10 minutes. In a large mixing bowl, place the whole-wheat flour, 1 cup of the unbleached flour, and salt. Mix in the hot water, oil, and honey. Beat until smooth. Add the dissolved yeast and beat well for about 10 minutes. Gradually add the remaining 1½ cups unbleached flour, sesame seeds, walnuts, and rosemary. Turn dough out onto a lightly floured board and knead lightly until smooth and elastic. Form into a rough ball, place in an oiled bowl, turn dough to coat top with oil, cover bowl, and let dough rise in a warm place until doubled in volume, about 1 hour.

Punch down dough and knead lightly on a floured board. Divide into 3 pieces. Shape each piece into a round or oblong loaf and place oblong loaves in greased 3½-by-7-inch loaf pans and round loaves on greased baking sheets. Cover loaves and let rise in a warm place until doubled in volume. Bake in a preheated 350° F. oven for 25 minutes, or until loaves sound hollow when thumped. Let cool on a wire rack 10 minutes, then remove from the pans. Makes 3 small loaves.

MENU

Smoked Trout
McDowell Dry Fumé Blanc

•

Chicken, Avocado, and Papaya Salad*
Brioche
McDowell Zinfandel Blanc

•

Strawberry Grenache Sorbet*

Chicken, Avocado, and Papaya Salad

Mango-Ginger Mayonnaise (recipe follows)

4 chicken breast halves (1½ to 2 pounds)

1 tablespoon safflower oil

Butter lettuce leaves

1 papaya

1 avocado

2 kiwi fruits

3 tablespoons roasted macadamia nuts, chopped

Prepare the Mango-Ginger Mayonnaise. Bone and skin chicken breasts and cut meat into long, thin strips. In a skillet placed over medium heat, heat oil and sauté chicken, stirring, until just cooked through, about 3 minutes. Remove to a plate from pan and let cool. Arrange a bed of lettuce on each of four dinner plates and mound chicken on the greens. Peel, seed, and slice papaya and avocado and arrange slices alongside chicken. Peel and slice kiwis and lay slices over chicken. Spoon mayonnaise dressing over the salad and sprinkle with nuts. Makes 4 servings.

Mango-Ginger Mayonnaise In a blender or a food processor fitted with a metal blade, combine ½ teaspoon dry mustard and 2 egg yolks and blend a few seconds. With motor running, add ⅔ cup grape-seed or safflower oil in a slow, steady stream, whirling until smooth and thick. Stir in 1 shallot, minced, 1 teaspoon grated orange peel, 1 teaspoon grated fresh ginger root, and ¼ cup each orange juice and chopped mango chutney. Thin with approximately ½ cup Zinfandel Blanc to desired dressing consistency. Chill.

Strawberry Grenache Sorbet

4 cups (2 pints) strawberries

2 cups Grenache Rosé wine

¾ cup granulated sugar

¼ cup orange juice

2 teaspoons grated lemon peel

2 egg whites

Mint sprigs for garnish

Purée berries in a blender or a food processor fitted with a metal blade. (You will need 2½ cups purée.) In a saucepan placed over medium heat, combine the wine and sugar and simmer, stirring, until sugar dissolves. Remove from the heat and cool. Stir in berry purée, orange juice, and lemon peel. Refrigerate until well chilled.

Whip egg whites until stiff but not dry and fold into chilled berry mixture. Pour into an ice-cream freezer and freeze following manufacturer's instructions. Spoon into long-stemmed goblets and garnish with mint sprigs. Makes 8 servings.

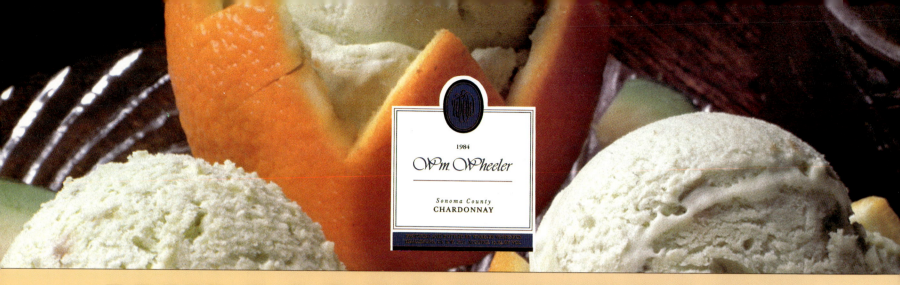

1984
Wm. Wheeler

Sonoma County
CHARDONNAY

WILLIAM WHEELER WINERY

Bill and Ingrid Wheeler are a handsome, active couple with an international background. They chose, however, to forgo a jet-set life style for wine making.

They met in Rio de Janeiro, when Bill was posted there in the foreign service and Ingrid was visiting her older brother. A slender, blond of Norwegian and Scottish ancestry, she had grown up in Hong Kong and France. They were married in London, England, lived in Brazil for a year, and then moved to Bogotá, Colombia, where their first child, Justin, was born. A daughter, Jessica, arrived in 1972.

While visiting friends in Healdsburg, California, in 1970, they fell in love with the area and purchased a 175-acre ranch. Giving up his job with an international venture-capital group, Bill apprenticed in France with Ingrid as "working guests" of Château Malescasse in Bordeux. They stayed for the 1971 harvest to learn how wine is made there, and then traveled to numerous wineries throughout Europe.

Returning with enthusiasm to California, the Wheelers began to clear the old vineyards and orchards that covered their acreage, an expanse of land that nestles between rolling hills eight hundred feet above the Dry Creek Valley floor. They planted Cabernet Sauvignon and named the area Norse Vineyards in honor of Ingrid's heritage.

Until 1979 they were grape growers, living and working in San Francisco during the week and in Healdsburg on weekends, physically accomplishing much of the development of the land through their own labor. They

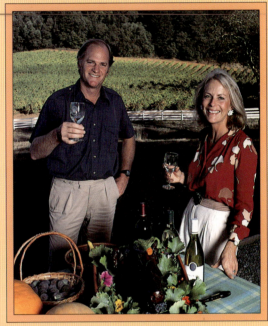

hired a wine maker and custom-crushed the 1979 and 1980 vintages with a mobile unit. Then in 1981 they moved to the area permanently and enrolled their children in school.

The winery office and aging room are located in a stylish renovated building off Healdsburg's downtown plaza. Plans are underway for a restaurant.

Their home and winery sit in a tranquil, panoramic setting. They often entertain at poolside, barbecuing salmon fillets or grilling game. Bill is famous for once capturing a wild boar with his bare hands, and sometimes boar is the star attraction at a Wheeler dinner. Their menus always combine continental flair with fresh California spirit.

Ingrid was born in Hong Kong to a Scottish mother and a Norwegian father who was in the shipping business. She was sent to boarding schools in England and Switzerland and finished her education at Cannes, where she spent weekends with her parents, who had moved to the south of France.

Wine was integral to dining at her parents' villa overlooking Monaco and the sparkling Mediterranean. She grew up savoring the grand old Bordeaux and Burgundies that her father locked away behind a grilled gate in the cellar.

Bill was born in St. Joseph, Missouri. There in the 1870s his great-grandfather started an outfitting company to supply the flood of pioneers passing through on their way west. He sold the business in the 1920s, but remained connected to the migrations through an extensive collection of western literature. Each book was stamped with his personal library seal, intertwined W's that are today the logo of the William Wheeler Winery.

The Wheelers rejoice in their endeavors. They have faced the great challenges posed by switching from a cosmopolitan life style to farming the land with serenity and poise. Dedicated and committed, they work as a team, always sharing equally in the tasks.

MENU
Catered by Jim Gibbons

TROUT AND SHRIMP MOUSSE*
WILLIAM WHEELER
SONOMA CHARDONNAY

•

DUCK WITH HOT PEACH HALVES*
CARROT AND CELERY ROOT NESTS
WITH BROCCOLI PURÉE*
CURLY ENDIVE SALAD
WILLIAM WHEELER
CABERNET SAUVIGNON

•

APPLE PITHIVIER*

Trout and Shrimp Mousse

1 pound sole or salmon fillets, chopped
3 egg whites
1 cup whipping cream
2 tablespoons each minced fresh parsley and chives
¼ teaspoon each salt and freshly ground black pepper
⅛ teaspoon freshly grated nutmeg
2 teaspoons Pernod liqueur
1 pound smoked trout or smoked salmon, chopped
6 ounces small cooked shrimp
Fresh lemon juice
Dorée Sauce (see Basic Recipes)

In a food processor fitted with a metal blade, purée the fresh fish to a coarse paste. Add egg whites and blend briefly. Add cream and blend to a fine paste. Transfer the mixture to a bowl and stir in parsley, chives, salt, pepper, nutmeg, Pernod, and smoked fish.

Butter 8 small ramekins (about ¾ cup each) and cover the bottoms with cooking parchment, cut to fit. Spoon half of the mousse mixture into the ramekins, filling each half full. Scatter the shrimp over the top and sprinkle with a few drops of lemon juice. Top with remaining mousse mixture. Place on each ramekin a buttered piece of parchment (buttered side down), cut to rest on top, and then cover with foil, pressing it down against the sides of the dish. Place ramekins on a rack in a baking pan containing hot water to reach halfway up the sides of the dishes. Bake in a preheated 325° F. oven for 20 minutes, or until a thin metal skewer inserted in center of mousse comes out clean.

While mousses are baking, prepare the Dorée Sauce. Remove the ramekins from the oven and let stand 10 minutes. Peel off foil and parchment, run a knife around the edge of each mousse to loosen it from the dish, and unmold onto serving plates. Serve warm or cold with the sauce. Makes 8 servings.

Duck with Hot Peach Halves

2 oranges
Water
2 ducklings with giblets (4 to 5 pounds each)
Salt and freshly ground black pepper
3 cups water
1 medium-size carrot, chopped
1 medium-size onion, chopped
1 tablespoon chicken stock base
½ cup Port wine
¼ cup currant jelly
2 tablespoons Cointreau or other orange-flavored liqueur
4 peaches
2 tablespoons granulated sugar

With a vegetable peeler, remove the peel from the oranges, being careful to get none of the white membrane. Place the peel in a saucepan, cover with water, bring to a boil, and simmer, covered, 15 minutes; drain. Cut the peel into julienne and set aside.

Prick ducks all over with two-tine fork, season with salt and pepper, and insert half the orange peel into the cavities. Place ducks on a rack in a roasting pan, breast side down. Roast in a preheated 400° F. oven for 30 minutes. Remove extra fat from drippings with a bulb baster. Pour 1 cup water into pan and add carrot and onion. Turn ducks breast up, reduce the heat to 350° F., and continue roasting 1 hour longer, or until legs move freely. Remove ducks to a platter and keep warm. Reserve pan drippings.

Meanwhile, place remaining 2 cups water, the stock base, and giblets in a saucepan. Cover and simmer about 1 hour; strain and place stock in a saucepan. Skim fat from roasting pan and add Port to drippings. Heat, stirring up crusty bits on pan bottom and then strain, discarding vegetables. Add strained drippings and jelly to stock, bring to a boil, and cook until slightly reduced, about 5 minutes. Add Cointreau and reserved orange peel and heat to serving temperature.

Peel, halve, and pit peaches. Lay peach halves, cut side up, on a foil-lined broiler pan. Sprinkle peaches with sugar and broil until heated through. Carve duck, arranging a leg or thigh and a portion of breast on each plate. Place a hot peach alongside each serving. Pass the sauce. Makes 8 servings.

Carrot and Celery Root Nests with Broccoli Purée

4 large carrots, cut into julienne
1 large celery root, peeled and cut into julienne
1 large bunch broccoli (about 1½ pounds)
½ cup whipping cream
4 tablespoons butter
Salt, freshly ground black pepper, and freshly grated nutmeg to taste

Immerse julienned carrots and celery root separately in boiling salted water until crisp-tender, about 3 minutes each; drain and cool in ice water; drain again. Toss the 2 vegetables together. On an oiled baking sheet, form julienned vegetables into 6 3½-inch "nests" with 2-inch-wide center pockets. Cover with foil and reheat in a preheated 325° F. oven for 15 minutes.

Meanwhile, trim broccoli and separate into flowerets. Cook in boiling salted water until very tender, about 8 minutes; drain. Put cooked broccoli in a blender or in a food processor fitted with a metal blade and purée until smooth, adding cream and butter once broccoli is broken up. Season with salt, pepper, and nutmeg. Spoon warm purée into the vegetable nests just before serving. Makes 8 servings.

Apple Pithivier

1 package (17 ounces) frozen puff pastry
6 Granny Smith apples or other green cooking apples, peeled, cored, and thinly sliced
6 tablespoons unsalted butter
¾ cup granulated sugar
2 eggs
1 cup blanched almonds, finely ground
1 tablespoon Calvados
Glaze: 1 egg, beaten with 1 tablespoon water

Thaw the pastry in the refrigerator. Divide the pastry in half. On a lightly floured board, roll out each half into a 10-inch round. Transfer 1 round to a baking sheet and reserve the second round on the board.

Place apples on a baking pan, dot with 1 tablespoon butter, and sprinkle with 3 tablespoons sugar. Bake in a preheated 450° F. oven for 10 to 12 minutes, or until apples are hot and start to look glazed. Let cool.

In a mixing bowl, beat together remaining 5 tablespoons butter and remaining sugar until well blended, then beat in eggs, one at a time. Mix in ground nuts and Calvados. Spread half the almond cream over the pastry on the baking sheet, leaving a 1-inch border around the edge. Arrange the cooked apples over the cream and top the apples with remaining almond cream. Brush uncovered edge with egg glaze and position second pastry round over almond cream layer. Press the edges of the 2 pastry rounds together to secure. Brush top pastry with egg glaze. With a knife tip, make a simple fanciful decoration on pastry, slashing through to the filling. Refrigerate 10 minutes to firm pastry, then bake in a preheated 400° F. oven for 20 to 25 minutes, or until golden brown. Serve warm, cut into wedges. Makes 8 to 10 servings.

MENU

CHILLED CHUTNEY MELON*
WILLIAM WHEELER SEMILLON

•

BARBECUED SALMON*
TENDER YOUNG GREENS AND
CHERRY TOMATOES WITH
VINAIGRETTE
SAUTÉED NEW POTATOES
DILL BREAD
WILLIAM WHEELER
SONOMA CHARDONNAY

•

ASSORTED CHEESES AND CRACKERS
WILLIAM WHEELER
CABERNET SAUVIGNON

•

BRAZILIAN AVOCADO ICE CREAM*

Chilled Chutney Melon

3 small to medium-size cantaloupes
¼ cup mayonnaise
¼ cup minced mango chutney
⅓ cup finely chopped toasted walnuts
Mint sprigs for garnish

Halve melons and remove and discard seeds. With a melon baller, scoop out as many balls as possible. Scrape out remaining flesh. Invert shells to drain. In a bowl, mix together the mayonnaise and chutney. Add the melon balls, stirring gently to coat well. Mix in the chopped nuts. Pile the melon balls into the melon shells and garnish with mint sprigs. Serve immediately. Makes 6 servings.

Barbecued Salmon

Tail end of half a salmon (about 2 pounds)
Vegetable oil
4 tablespoons butter
¼ cup fresh lemon juice
½ teaspoon dried tarragon, crumbled
¼ teaspoon freshly ground black pepper
2 shallots, chopped

Remove tail and fins from salmon. Butterfly salmon by cutting along the stomach, or underside, to the tail. Flatten the fish as much as possible. Brush both sides of fish with oil and place in a hinged barbecue basket. Melt butter in a small pan and stir in lemon juice, tarragon, pepper, and shallots. Place fish on a grill over a medium-hot fire. (If you don't have a basket, put fish directly on grill, skin side down.) Basting frequently with butter mixture, grill salmon, turning once, until it barely flakes when tested with a fork, about 10 to 12 minutes. Makes 6 servings.

Brazilian Avocado Ice Cream

1 large avocado
¾ cup granulated sugar
¼ cup fresh lemon juice
½ cup thawed undiluted orange juice concentrate
1 teaspoon grated lemon peel
1 cup whipping cream

Peel and pit avocado and mash well (you should have ¾ cup). In a bowl, combine avocado, sugar, lemon juice, and orange concentrate and stir until blended. Mix in lemon peel. Pour into a shallow pan and freeze for 30 minutes. Remove from freezer and whirl in a food processor fitted with a metal blade until thick and fluffy (or beat with an electric mixer). Whip cream until stiff and gently fold into avocado mixture. Turn into a freezer container or individual soufflé dishes, and freeze until set, about 1 hour. Makes 6 servings.

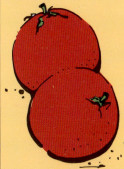

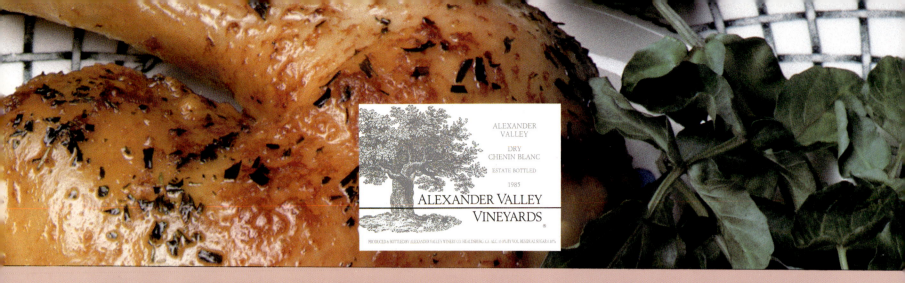

ALEXANDER VALLEY
VINEYARDS

Alexander Valley Vineyards sits on a beautiful historic estate alongside the Russian River. Maggie and Harry Wetzel of Palo Verdes, California, purchased the property in the early 1960s as a summer and weekend retreat for their family of four children.

At the time, the rundown Victorian house was masked by five-foot-tall weeds. The front porch was boarded up and steers poked their heads through the windows. Now lovingly restored, the big white home with its gingerbread trim is surrounded by a sweeping veranda. Among the furnishings are showpiece antiques. Striking appliquéd quilted bedspreads cover the four-posters and dear wooden cradles stand ready for rocking. With the Wetzels' ten grandchildren, they have come in handy.

The house was built in 1842 by Cyrus Alexander, an early Euro-American settler who made a fortune growing produce and selling it in San Francisco. Following the 1906 earthquake, woodwork was added to the original adobe structure. Later abandoned, the home fell into neglect and squatters settled on the adjacent property.

On a nearby knoll stands an 1868 white schoolhouse, refurbished as an idyllic guest retreat. From the beginning, Maggie was determined to preserve this nineteenth-century trea-

sure. She had it moved from its original location half a mile away, where it had long served as a hay barn once its days as an institution of learning had passed. Now polished and spacious, it is one huge room with a kitchen

sidebar and bedroom balcony. Tiger rugs and heads accent the wood floors and walls, mementos of Harry's big-game safaris in Africa.

The bell still hangs in the belfry overhead, a symbol of the building's importance to children and church goers for over a century.

While the main house was being papered and painted, its grounds were slowly cleared of debris and transformed into a beautiful landscape. Vineyards were planted and a vegetable garden was added close to the home and pool.

In 1975 construction on the winery commenced, following the Wetzel children's expression of interest in wine making. Hank Wetzel III had just earned a degree in oenology from the University of California, Davis, and building a winery seemed the next logical step. Today he is the wine maker and general manager, and his younger sister, Katie Wetzel Murphy, serves as national sales manager. The operation is presently undergoing extensive expansion.

Maggie and Harry are involved in the cultural activities of Los Angeles, serving on music and art councils. Harry is chairman of the board of Garrett Corporation, a manufacturer of aircraft equipment.

Mother and daughter are look-alikes and often work as a team in entertaining. Picnics and luncheons are held alfresco, under the shade of a big Astrakhan apple tree. Most menus revolve around the abundance in the vegetable garden and the fruits from the ancient trees that surround the home.

The storybook home and picturesque acreage make an idyllic setting for family gatherings and convivial guest parties.

MENU

TOASTED BAGUETTES WITH CHÈVRE
AND SUN-DRIED TOMATOES*
TARRAGON CHICKEN*
LIMA BEAN, TOMATO, AND
RED ONION SALAD*
ALEXANDER VALLEY CHARDONNAY

•

NECTARINES AND BLUEBERRIES
WITH PLUM SAUCE*

Toasted Baguettes with Chèvre and Sun-dried Tomatoes

1 baguette
Olive oil
6 ounces chèvre or mozzarella cheese
16 sun-dried tomatoes
Basil leaves

Thinly slice the baguette into 16 slices and brush each slice lightly with oil. Spread each slice with a thin layer of chèvre or top with a thin slice of mozzarella. Arrange 1 dried tomato on top of each baguette slice and top each tomato with a leaf of basil. Bake in a preheated 450° F. oven for 8 to 10 minutes, or until thoroughly heated. Makes 16, 8 servings.

Tarragon Chicken

2 broiler-fryer chickens (about 3 pounds each), halved
4 tablespoons butter
3 tablespoons Dijon-style mustard
2 tablespoons fresh tarragon leaves, or 1½ teaspoons dried tarragon, crumbled

Arrange the chicken halves, skin side up, in a baking dish. In a small saucepan placed over low heat, combine the butter and mustard and heat, stirring, until blended. With a pastry brush, evenly coat each chicken half with the butter-mustard mixture and then sprinkle with tarragon leaves. Bake in a preheated 375° F. oven for 45 minutes to 1 hour, or until cooked through and juices no longer run pink when thigh joint is pierced. Cut each chicken half in half again and arrange on a serving platter. Makes 8 servings.

Lima Bean, Tomato, and Red Onion Salad

Tarragon Vinaigrette (recipe follows)
2 quarts water
Salt
4 cups shelled fresh lima beans, or 3 packages (10 ounces each) frozen lima beans
1 red onion
1 cup small yellow Italian plum tomatoes or cherry tomatoes, halved

Prepare the Tarragon Vinaigrette. In a large saucepan, bring the water to a boil and salt lightly. Add lima beans and boil rapidly until beans are tender, about 15 to 20 minutes for fresh limas and 7 to 8 minutes for frozen ones. Drain in a colander and turn into a bowl. While the beans are still hot, pour the vinaigrette over them. Thinly slice the onion, separate the slices into rings, and toss with the limas. Scatter the tomatoes over the top, cover, and chill. Toss gently just before serving. Makes 8 servings.

Tarragon Vinaigrette

In a jar with a tight-fitting lid, combine ¼ teaspoon each salt, dry mustard, medium-cracked black pepper, and granulated sugar, and 3 tablespoons each tarragon wine vinegar, safflower oil, and olive oil. Twist lid onto jar and shake well.

Nectarines and Blueberries with Plum Sauce

2½ cups Plum Sauce (recipe follows)
2 tablespoons framboise liqueur
4 nectarines or peaches
2 cups (1 pint) blueberries or raspberries

Prepare the Plum Sauce. Place 2½ cups of the sauce in a saucepan and heat slightly. Stir in liqueur.

Plunge nectarines into boiling water for approximately 30 seconds, or until skins loosen. Drain, peel, halve, and pit. (If using peaches, treat in the same manner.) Place each nectarine half in a wine goblet, cut side up. Center each nectarine half with berries. Surround fruit with a shallow pool of sauce and pass remaining sauce in a pitcher. Makes 8 servings.

Plum Sauce Place 2 pounds whole red plums, such as Santa Rosas or Duartes, in a large saucepan. Cook gently over low heat, stirring occasionally, for 20 to 25 minutes, or until softened. Bring to a boil over medium-high heat and let juices boil 1 minute. Remove from the heat, cool slightly, and then press plums and juices through a food mill placed over a bowl. Discard skins and seeds that collect in the mill. Sweeten the purée with 3 to 4 tablespoons mild-flavored honey, or to taste. If desired, make the sauce in quantity and freeze in small jars or freezer containers.

MENU

GLAZED BAKED HAM*
ASSORTED MUSTARDS AND CHUTNEYS
NEW POTATO AND MINT SALAD*
CUCUMBERS VINAIGRETTE
ALEXANDER VALLEY CHENIN BLANC
AND GEWÜRZTRAMINER
•
ESTATE-GROWN APPLESAUCE*
ALMOND BARS*

Glazed Baked Ham

**Half of a cured,
  smoked, fully
  cooked ham (4 to 5
  pounds)**
Apple juice
Raw sugar
Whole cloves
**Assorted mustards
  and chutneys**

Remove any remaining skin from ham and score the fat in diamond shapes. Place ham cut side down on a rack in a roasting pan and insert a meat thermometer in the thickest portion. Pour a little apple juice over the ham and rub it into the surface of the ham with some raw sugar. Stick a whole clove in the center of each scored diamond. Bake in a preheated 350° F. oven for 1½ hours or until the thermometer registers 130° F. Let ham cool to room temperature. Slice and serve with assorted mustards and chutneys. Makes 8 or more servings.

New Potato and Mint Salad

**16 small red new
  potatoes**
⅓ cup olive oil
**Salt and freshly
  ground black
  pepper to taste**
**¼ cup chopped fresh
  mint leaves, or ½
  cup chopped
  watercress leaves**

Steam potatoes in their skins until just tender. Remove them from the steamer and slice into a bowl while still warm. Pour on the olive oil and season with salt and pepper. Toss gently and then cool to room temperature. When ready to serve, add mint and mix lightly. Makes 8 servings.

Estate-Grown Applesauce

**2 pounds Astrakhan,
  Jonathan, or Granny
  Smith apples**
1 cup water
**½ cup mild-flavored
  honey**
Freshly grated nutmeg
**Whipping cream or
  half-and-half for
  serving**

Quarter, peel, and seed apples. Place in a large kettle, add water, and cover kettle with a tight-fitting lid. Place over low heat and cook apples, stirring every 30 minutes, until soft and fruit will mash with a potato masher, about 1 to 1¼ hours. Remove kettle from the heat, mash the apples until no lumps remain, sweeten with honey. Stir in nutmeg. Let cool to room temperature and serve plain or with cream. Makes 8 to 10 servings.

Almond Bars

**½ pound (1 cup)
  unsalted butter, at
  room temperature**
**¾ cup sifted
  confectioners' sugar**
**2 teaspoons vanilla
  extract**
**1 teaspoon almond
  extract**
**1 cup blanched
  almonds, ground**
**2½ cups sifted
  unbleached flour**
**Confectioners' sugar
  for topping
  (optional)**

In a mixing bowl, cream butter until light and fluffy and beat in sifted sugar. Add vanilla extract, almond extract, and ground almonds and mix well. With your hands, knead sifted flour into butter-sugar mixture until well combined. Wrap the dough in plastic and chill 1 hour.

Place dough on a lightly floured board and roll out into a sheet about ½ inch thick. Using a knife or pastry cutter, cut dough into bars or crescents. Transfer cutouts to a greased baking sheet and bake in a preheated 350° F. oven for 15 minutes, or until lightly browned. Transfer bars to a wire rack to cool. If desired, sift a light dusting of confectioners' sugar over the bars while they are still warm. Store in an airtight tin. Makes about 3 dozen.

1984
Napa Valley
FUMÉ BLANC
Dry Sauvignon Blanc
ALCOHOL 12.5% BY VOLUME
PRODUCED AND BOTTLED BY
ROBERT MONDAVI WINERY
OAKVILLE, CALIFORNIA

ROBERT MONDAVI WINERY

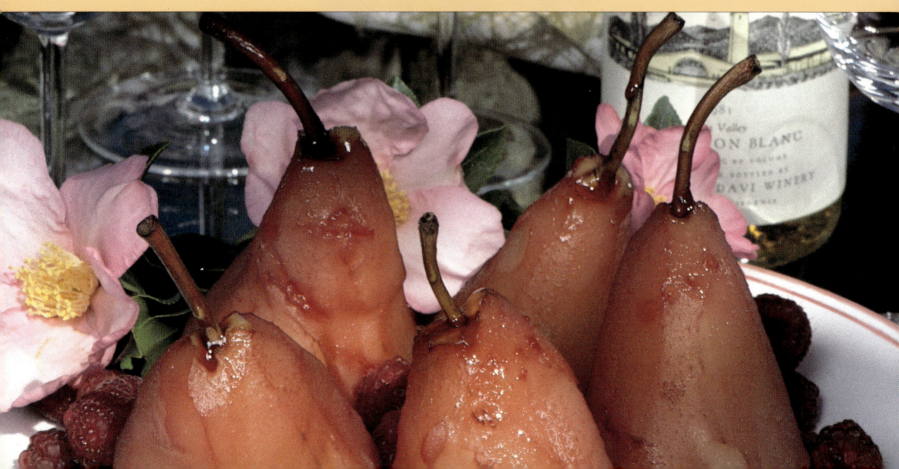

At their spectacular hilltop home overlooking Napa Valley, Robert Mondavi and his wife, Margrit Biever, enjoy a few moments of privacy. Perhaps they share an early morning tennis match, or a chèvre pizza picnic under the buckeye trees on nearby Wappo Hill, a historic Indian reservation.

The Robert Mondavi Winery sponsors a wide-ranging program of educational courses, including the Great Chefs of France and America cooking schools, harvest and oak aging seminars, and a comprehensive winery-tour program. Monthly art shows and annual summer jazz festivals have become traditions.

At a cooking-school event, students receive first-hand instruction from such famous chefs as Julia Child, Alice Waters, and Paul Prudhomme. Swiss-born Margrit, who is fluent in many languages, translates for visiting continental luminaries like Paul Bocuse, Alain Chapel, Roger Vergé, and Pierre Troisgros.

A stylish, multitalented woman, Margrit delights in cooking in her new tile-lined home kitchen, turning out loaves of seven-grain bread or raspberry-garlanded poached pears. It is likely she will mix a luncheon pizza dough in tandem with preparing breakfast. Juggling several activities and a coterie of guests comes naturally to her.

When it comes to food, Robert says, "I like combinations that are right and good. You don't have to bring in the offbeat. The more natural and simple the food, the better I like the menus. With our wines, we're developing a style of drinkability and character, actually sculpturing the wines to enhance food."

The Robert Mondavi Winery was founded in 1966, the culmination of a vision Robert shared with his family.

In 1910 Robert's parents, Cesare and Rosa Mondavi, emigrated from the Marches region of Italy to Minnesota, where Robert was born in 1913. His father became involved in purchasing and shipping California wine grapes to fellow Italian emigres in the Midwest. This demanded frequent trips to California.

The family moved to Lodi in 1923, where the elder Mondavi set up an ambitious fruit-shipping firm. Robert recalls long hours spent helping his father transform grapes into wine for the family table.

Robert graduated from Stanford University in 1936 with a degree in economics. He then joined his father in the wine business and studied oenology. Soon he began to develop his own convictions on the potential of Napa Valley wines, and aimed to upgrade the technique and technology of the family enterprise, to move beyond the production of bulk wines.

His big chance came when the old Charles Krug Winery was offered for sale and he convinced his father to purchase it. They began replanting the vineyards with the finest varietals and upgrading the vinification techniques.

Then Robert left the Charles Krug operation to start his own winery. He was the first Napa Valley vintner to utilize cold fermentation extensively. He was also responsible for single-handedly popularizing new styles of wine, such as Chenin Blanc and Fumé Blanc. He introduced blind tastings, realizing "that mass advertising for fine wines wasn't the best way to sell wines."

Today the wholly-owned family enterprise produces varietals and premium table wines totaling 1.4 million cases annually. A joint venture with the Baron Philippe de Rothschild of Château Mouton Rothschild produces a Napa Valley Cabernet combining French vinification techniques with American technical expertise.

The winery has always stood for innovation and high quality and is a leader in anticipating and setting new trends. Robert Mondavi plays a major role in the California wine industry.

MENU

CALIFORNIA CHÈVRE PIZZAS*
SALAD OF ASSORTED GREENS
ROBERT MONDAVI FUMÉ BLANC

•

POACHED PEARS WITH RASPBERRIES*
ROBERT MONDAVI MOSCATO D'ORO

California Chèvre Pizzas

1 package active dry yeast (scant 1 tablespoon)
1 cup lukewarm water (110° F.)
¼ cup whole-wheat or rye flour
1 tablespoon milk
2 tablespoons olive oil
½ teaspoon salt
1¾ cups unbleached flour
1 teaspoon each chopped fresh rosemary and thyme
1 clove garlic, minced
1 can (6 ounces) tomato paste
4 or 5 tomatoes, sliced ¼ inch thick
2 cups shredded Provolone cheese (about ½ pound)
2 red or green bell peppers, seeded and cut into strips
½ cup chopped fresh parsley
4 green onions, chopped
¾ pound California chèvre or imported buffalo mozzarella, cut into 1-inch chunks
Garlic-flavored olive oil
1 tablespoon fresh lemon juice

In a mixing bowl, sprinkle yeast into ½ cup lukewarm water and let stand until dissolved and foamy, about 10 minutes. Stir in whole-wheat flour, cover bowl, and let dough rise for 30 minutes. Add the remaining ½ cup lukewarm water, the milk, olive oil, salt, and 1 cup unbleached flour and beat with a dough hook or by hand until smooth. Mix in the remaining ¾ cup unbleached flour, beating well until dough pulls away from the sides of the bowl. Turn dough out onto a lightly floured board and knead 1 minute. Form into a rough ball, place in an oiled bowl, turn dough to oil top, cover bowl, and let dough rise 1½ hours, or until doubled in volume. Punch down, divide in half, and on a lightly floured board roll each portion into a 12-inch round. With fingertips, press rounds into oiled pizza pans.

Mix rosemary, thyme, and garlic into tomato paste and spread over the dough rounds. Cover with sliced tomatoes and sprinkle with Provolone, pepper strips, parsley, and green onions. Dot with 1-inch chunks of chèvre. Drizzle with a few drops of garlic-flavored olive oil and sprinkle with lemon juice. Bake in a 500° F. preheated oven for 8 minutes, or until the crust is golden. Makes 6 servings.

Poached Pears with Raspberries

6 Anjou, Bosc, or Comice pears
2 cups Pinot Noir
1 cup water
¾ cup granulated sugar
1 2-inch cinnamon stick
2 thin slices fresh ginger root
1 lemon
2 cups (1 pint) raspberries

With a potato peeler or a small knife, carefully core the pears, working from the bottom and leaving the stems intact. Peel pears and stand them upright in a saucepan. Add wine, water, sugar, cinnamon stick, and ginger slices to the saucepan. Cut the lemon in half, squeeze the juice over the pears, and add the lemon halves to the pan. Bring to a boil, lower the heat, cover, and simmer until pears are just tender but still firm, about 15 to 20 minutes. Remove pears from the pan to a platter. Boil poaching liquid to reduce to about ¼ cup. Cool pears and syrup completely. At serving time, drizzle syrup over pears and ring with raspberries. Makes 6 servings.

MENU

ASPARAGUS WITH LEMON BUTTER
AND TOASTED PINE NUTS
ROBERT MONDAVI FUMÉ BLANC

•

VITELLO TONNATO (VEAL WITH
TUNA SAUCE*)
RISOTTO*
GOLDEN SUMMER SQUASH
WITH BLOSSOMS
ROBERT MONDAVI CHARDONNAY

•

CURLY ENDIVE SALAD WITH
BAVARIAN BLUE

•

RASPBERRY SORBET WITH NECTARINE
FAN AND TINY GRAPES*
ROBERT MONDAVI
SAUVIGNON BLANC BOTRYTIS

Vitello Tonnato (Veal with Tuna Sauce)

1 boneless veal roast
    (about 3 pounds)
Salt and freshly
    ground black
    pepper
Mayonnaise (recipe
    follows)
1 can (6 ounces)
    white albacore tuna
    packed in oil
1 cup olive oil
3 canned anchovy
    fillets
2 tablespoons fresh
    lemon juice
1½ teaspoons capers,
    drained

1 teaspoon red-wine
    vinegar
Fresh herbs for gar-
    nish, such as
    oregano, basil, or
    tarragon

Place the roast on a rack in a roasting pan and season with salt and pepper. Insert a meat thermometer in the thickest portion of the roast and cook the meat in a preheated 325° F. oven until medium rare, about 1 hour, or until the thermometer registers 145° F. Remove the roast from the oven, let cool, and chill.

To make the tuna sauce, first prepare the Mayonnaise. Then place the tuna and its oil, olive oil, anchovies, lemon juice, capers, and vinegar in a blender or a food processor fitted with a metal blade and blend until smooth. Gently mix in the Mayonnaise.

Slice chilled roast into ⅜-inch-thick slices. Spoon some of the sauce over a large platter and arrange meat slices on it. Coat top of meat with a thin layer of sauce. Cover and refrigerate at least 24 hours before serving. Garnish with herbs. Makes 8 servings.

Mayonnaise Place in a blender or a food processor fitted with a metal blade 1 egg, 1 egg yolk, ½ teaspoon Sherry vinegar or white-wine vinegar, 2 tablespoons fresh lemon juice, and a pinch of salt. Blend a few seconds. With motor running, gradually add 1¼ to 1½ cups olive oil in a slow, steady steam. Continue to blend until thickened to desired consistency.

Risotto

1 medium onion,
    finely chopped
¼ cup unsalted butter
1½ cups Italian
    arborio rice
1 quart chicken stock
½ cup Fumè Blanc or
    dry white wine
Pinch saffron
    (optional)
½ cup grated
    Parmesan cheese
Salt and pepper
    to taste

In a large saucepan saute onion in butter until transparent. Add rice and saute until kernels are glazed. Separately bring stock to a boil in a saucepan. Add one ladleful of stock to the rice and stir until stock is absorbed. Repeat with another ladleful of stock as rice dries. Add wine and saffron to rice and continue to cook and stir, until liquid is absorbed. Repeat with remaining stock. When rice is done but al dente, add cheese and salt and pepper to taste and mix lightly with a fork. makes 6 servings.

Raspberry Sorbet with Nectarine Fan and Tiny Grapes

1 cup granulated sugar
1½ cups water
4 cups (2 pints)
    raspberries
1 tablespoon fram-
    boise or kirsch
    liqueur (optional)
3 nectarines, peeled,
    pitted, and sliced
6 clusters of tiny
    seedless grapes

In a saucepan, combine the sugar and water, bring to a boil, stirring, and boil for 5 minutes. Remove from the heat and let cool. Purée raspberries in a blender, or food processor fitted with a metal blade, then press through a sieve, discarding seeds. (There should be about 2½ cups of purée.) Add berry purée to the cool syrup and stir in framboise, if desired. Pour into an ice-cream freezer and freeze following manufacturer's instructions.

To serve, place one scoop of sorbet on each dessert plate. Arrange around each scoop nectarine slices, arranged in a fan shape, and a grape cluster. Makes 6 servings, about 1½ quarts.

ESTATE BOTTLED

IRON HORSE
VINEYARDS™

Steep, rocky vineyards and the cool, coastal climate (Region 1) of Western Sonoma County give Iron Horse Chardonnays their consistent style: aromatic in the nose, supple in body, crisp, almost flinty in the finish. Due to the growing conditions in 1984, the wine has a rich full texture, balanced with good acidity, giving it great finesse. Bottle bouquet will intensify with extended bottle age.

The grapes for this 100% Chardonnay wine were hand picked in the second week of September. After 12 hours skin contact, 65% of the wine was fermented in small French oak barrels, and the remainder in French and Yugoslavian oak upright tanks. The lots were kept separate and aged 4 months in French oak barrels. After blending, 6000 cases were bottled in early July, 1985.

1984
Sonoma County-Green Valley
Chardonnay

GROWN, PRODUCED & BOTTLED BY IRON HORSE VINEYARDS
SEBASTOPOL, CALIFORNIA, USA • ALCOHOL 13.5% BY VOLUME

IRON HORSE VINEYARDS

Early spring at Iron Horse Vineyards is a golden experience. More than thirty-two thousand daffodils cover the landscaped approach to the restored nineteenth-century home of Audrey and Barry Sterling. As the seasons progress, the palette of flowers turns to hot pinks in summer, then softer burnt orange in autumn.

The ten acres of landscaped and terraced gardens are a showplace. A vast assortment of vegetables and herbs are intermingled. "Flowers are my passion," says Audrey. Two greenhouses on the property provide year-round abundance for her hobby.

Together with Forrest Tancer, the Sterlings are partners in Iron Horse, and while Forrest makes the wines, Audrey oversees the gustatory delights that accompany them.

Her fame as a hostess has gained her national renown. Inspiration for many of her dishes comes from extensive travel and from living abroad. She has amassed a vast collection of china and crystal that she regularly integrates into the five-course meal that is *de rigueur* for home dining.

Until recently she did all the cooking, but now she is happily assisted in the kitchen by Burmese-born Katherine Htim, who sets forth exciting Oriental fare that combines splendidly with Iron Horse sparkling and still wines.

When the Sterlings purchased the property in 1976, Audrey had not cooked for twenty-five years, as they had always had a kitchen staff. At that time it was difficult to hire a cook in Sonoma, prompting Barry to point out, "Either you have to learn to cook or you'd better lower your standards."

Audrey accepted the challenge and became a talented chef, holding parties at their California home and ex-

perimenting for just the two of them in their fourteenth-century house in the south of France.

Her striking table settings and menus are often featured in national magazines. In 1985 Iron Horse's sparkling Blanc de Blancs gained international fame when it was poured at the Gorbachev-Reagan Summit dinner in Geneva.

The Sterlings both grew up in California. Barry entered Stanford University at age sixteen and passed the bar examination before graduation from law school at age twenty-two. He married Audrey, a classmate, and they moved to Washington, D.C., where he worked at the Pentagon. Upon completing his two-year military duty, they returned to Los Angeles, where he practiced corporate law and founded his own firm by 1960.

His first trip to Europe, a thirtieth birthday gift from Audrey, began years of travel abroad for business and pleasure. They both fell in love with France and vowed to live there.

In 1966 Barry joined an international law practice in Paris. Their apartment had a wine cave with space for ten thousand bottles, encouraging Barry to launch a tasting program, for which he collected more than four thousand European vintages.

They searched for seven years for a French château where they could serve fine food and make estate wines. Discouraged by appellation problems, they returned to California and, following a close look at the potential of the state's wines, renewed their search for a vineyard, this time in Sonoma County. They first saw Iron Horse Ranch in a driving rainstorm. Although it needed extensive renovations, it offered all they had been seeking.

Once a railroad stop, for which it was named, the three-hundred-acre Iron Horse sits on the crest of a knoll in Green Valley. The iron-horse logo appears throughout the property and the ranch's generic wine bears the name Tin Pony.

For the first eight years the Sterlings owned the ranch, Barry continued to serve at his Los Angeles firm, flying north only on weekends. Since 1984 he has been on hand full-time to oversee the management.

MENU

ORIENTAL EGGPLANT SALAD*
GINGERED CUCUMBER SALAD*
CHICKEN CURRY*
POACHED PRUNES IN
IRON HORSE BRUT*
IRON HORSE BRUT SPARKLING WINE

Oriental Eggplant Salad

1 medium-size eggplant
3 slices fresh ginger root
3 cloves garlic
1 tablespoon Oriental-style sesame oil
2 tablespoons rice-wine vinegar
1 to 1½ teaspoons granulated sugar
1 teaspoon soy sauce
1 teaspoon paprika
Minced cilantro for garnish

Cut unpeeled eggplant in half and place on an oiled baking sheet. Bake in a preheated 350° F. oven for 30 minutes, or until tender. Let eggplant halves cool slightly and then peel off the skin. Let cool completely, cut each half into 5 or 6 lengthwise sections, and place in a bowl.

For the dressing, place the ginger root and garlic in a blender and whirl to mince. Add sesame oil, vinegar, sugar, soy, and paprika and blend thoroughly. Pour dressing over eggplant and chill 1 hour or longer to blend flavors. Garnish with coriander. Makes 4 to 6 servings.

Gingered Cucumber Salad

2 large cucumbers, peeled, halved, seeded, and thinly sliced
1 large red onion, thinly sliced
1 bunch radishes, trimmed and thinly sliced
1 red bell pepper, seeded and cut into long, thin strips
2 teaspoons chopped fresh cilantro
1 tablespoon finely grated fresh ginger root
1 cup rice-wine vinegar
Cilantro springs for garnish

In a serving bowl, combine the cucumbers, onion, radishes, pepper strips, chopped cilantro, and ginger. Pour vinegar over vegetables and mix lightly. Cover and chill until serving time. Garnish with cilantro sprigs. Makes 4 to 6 servings.

Chicken Curry

1 broiler-fryer chicken (about 3½ pounds), cut into 8 serving pieces
1 teaspoon salt
2 tablespoons curry powder
1 cup milk or coconut milk (see Note)
3 tablespoons safflower oil
2 medium-size onions, finely chopped
2 cloves garlic, minced
2 bay leaves
1 teaspoon minced fresh ginger root
Salt and freshly ground black pepper to taste

Place chicken pieces in a large bowl. Combine salt, curry powder, and milk, pour over chicken, and marinate for 1 hour.

In a heavy saucepan, heat oil over medium heat, add onions, garlic, bay leaves, and ginger, and sauté until onions are transparent, about 5 minutes. Drain chicken, reserving marinade. Add chicken to pan and cook until browned, turning pieces often, about 10 minutes. Add the reserved marinade to the pan and cook over medium-high heat, covered, for 10 minutes, or until the chicken is tender and the sauce is thickened. Season with salt and pepper. Makes 4 servings.

Note: *Coconut milk is available canned in Southeast Asian markets and some supermarkets.*

Poached Prunes in Iron Horse Brut

1 fifth Brut Sparkling Wine
Peel of 1 lemon
¾ cup granulated sugar
1 vanilla bean, split lengthwise
3 2-inch cinnamon sticks
30 dried prunes
Whipping cream
Confectioners' sugar and ground ginger or chopped candied ginger to taste

In a saucepan, combine the wine, lemon peel, sugar, vanilla bean, and cinnamon sticks. Bring to a boil and simmer, stirring to dissolve sugar, 5 minutes. Add prunes and poach over low heat until just tender, about 20 to 25 minutes. Remove prunes with a slotted spoon to a serving dish. Boil poaching liquid over high heat to reduce to 1½ cups. Remove lemon peel, cinnamon, and vanilla bean and pour sauce over prunes. Serve at room temperature with cream flavored with sugar and ginger. Makes 4 to 6 servings.

MENU

GARLIC AND CHESTNUT SOUP*
IRON HORSE FUMÉ BLANC

•

**VEAL SAUSAGE AND NEW POTATOES
POACHED IN CHARDONNAY***
IRON HORSE CHARDONNAY

•

GREEN SALAD AND AGED CHÈVRE
IRON HORSE CABERNET SAUVINGON

•

**TIN PONY WIND CAKE
WITH MOCHA FROSTING***
IRON HORSE BLANC DE PINOT NOIR
SPARKING WINE

Garlic and Chestnut Soup

3 tablespoons unsalted butter
1 large onion, chopped
½ cup garlic cloves, minced
2 cups chicken stock
1 can (15 ounces) unsweetened whole chestnuts, with liquid
1 cup Fumé Blanc or other dry white wine
Freshly grated nutmeg to taste
Whipped cream for garnish

In a large saucepan placed over medium heat, melt the butter, add onions, and sauté until transparent, about 5 minutes. Add garlic and sauté a few seconds. Add stock and chestnuts with liquid, bring to a boil, and simmer 15 minutes, or until garlic is soft. Cool slightly, then purée until smooth in a blender or in a food processor fitted with a metal blade. Return purée to the saucepan and add wine. Simmer for 5 minutes and add nutmeg. Ladle soup into individual bowls and top each serving with a dollop of whipped cream. Makes 6 servings.

Veal Sausage and New Potatoes Poached in Chardonnay

2 tablespoons butter
6 veal sausages, such as bratwurst or bockwurst (about 2 pounds)
1 large onion, chopped
1 cup Chardonnay or other dry white wine
1 cup chicken stock
1 clove garlic, minced
Chopped fresh basil, lemon thyme, and oregano to taste
1 tablespoon tomato paste
1 pound small new potatoes, peeled and halved
1 cup sliced zucchini
Chopped fresh parsley for garnish

In a dutch oven, melt the butter. Lightly brown the sausages in the butter and, at the same time, sauté the onion alongside. Pour in the wine and chicken stock and add garlic, herbs, tomato paste, and potatoes. Bring to a boil, reduce the heat to low, cover, and simmer gently 10 minutes. Remove sausages and keep warm. Continue cooking potatoes until they are almost tender, about 5 minutes longer. Add zucchini and simmer until just tender, about 3 minutes. Return sausage to pan and heat through. Sprinkle with parsley. Makes 6 servings.

Tin Pony Wind Cake with Mocha Frosting

6 eggs, separated
¼ teaspoon salt
¾ teaspoon cream of tartar
½ cup water
1⅓ cups granulated sugar
1 teaspoon vanilla extract
1½ cups sifted cake flour
Mocha Frosting (recipe follows)

In a mixing bowl, beat egg whites with an electric mixer until foamy. Add salt and cream of tartar, and beat until stiff but not dry. Set aside. In another bowl, beat egg yolks at medium speed for 1 minute. Add water and beat for 1 minute longer. Continuing to beat, gradually add sugar. When sugar is completely incorporated, beat mixture for 10 minutes at high speed. Mix in vanilla extract.

Sift flour before measuring and then sift again. Mix flour into the yolk mixture. Stir one-third of the whites into the yolk mixture to lighten it, then gently fold in remaining whites. Turn batter into an ungreased 10-inch tube pan with removable bottom. Cut through batter with a knife blade a few times to break large air bubbles. Place pan in center of oven on low rack and bake in a preheated 350° F. oven for 40 minutes, or until cake springs back when touched lightly. Invert pan on a wire rack and let cool completely. Remove cake from pan. Make Mocha Frosting and frost top and sides of cake. Makes 12 servings.

Mocha Frosting Place in a mixing bowl 4 tablespoons butter, at room temperature, 2 tablespoons unsweetened cocoa powder, ¾ teaspoon instant-coffee granules, and ½ teaspoon vanilla extract and mix until well blended. Add 1 egg and beat until smooth. Gradually add 2 cups confectioners' sugar, beating until mixture forms a good spreading consistency. If necessary, add 1 or 2 teaspoons water to thin to desired consistency.

RUTHERFORD HILL

1982
Napa Valley
MERLOT

PRODUCED AND BOTTLED BY RUTHERFORD HILL WINERY
RUTHERFORD, CALIF., USA • ALCOHOL 13.0% BY VOLUME

RUTHERFORD HILL WINERY

In 1965 Bill and Lila Jaeger yearned for an old Victorian house in the wine country as a weekend retreat. The first day they looked they found it! It was an 1864 yellow gingerbread-trimmed home with a great veranda, regally sited in St. Helena at the end of a vineyard-lined lane.

It wasn't long before Bill, an Oakland, California attorney, and his family moved to the Napa Valley. Over the years the Jaegers have transformed the grounds into a showplace. In 1970 they built a guesthouse, a charming replica of the Victorian era. It is not unusual for a television crew to move in, to film a sequence for a commercial.

Bill's career in wine embraces several aspects of the industry, beginning with the founding of Freemark Abbey Winery in 1967. In 1971 he began developing Curtis Ranches, one of the largest vineyard operations in the valley. Then in 1976 he became the organizing founder of Rutherford Hill. Today he operates a third cellar, the Jaeger Family Company, which produces about five thousand cases a year.

The Jaegers' three sons, Bill, Jeff, and Jack, all work in the wine business: in marketing, running vineyards, or making oak barrels. Daughter Betsy Morgenthaler has just blessed them with their third grandchild and first grandson.

Rutherford Hill Winery was founded as a partnership of growers, experienced wine people, and friends. Located in the Napa Valley on a hillside east of Rutherford, its exterior resembles an Early American

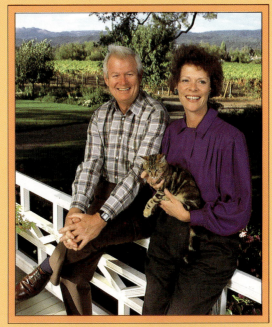

hay barn: the weathered wood blends harmoniously with surrounding trees and knolls. The winery's focus has always been on producing premium bottlings of excellent quality and value, wines that add to dining pleasure.

Both Bill and Lila are native Californians. Bill graduated from Hastings College of Law, San Francisco, and was administrative assistant to William F. Knowland, majority leader of the United States Senate from 1952 to 1954. Leaving Washington, he practiced law in Oakland and Piedmont until 1970.

Currently, he is director and chairman of the board of World Neighbors, an international organization based in Oklahoma City that helps the impoverished attain self-sufficiency, and a member of numerous wine groups.

During her thirty-five years of marriage to Bill, Lila has acquired a vast repertoire of favorite dishes for family and guests. Today her trend is to homey fare like stuffed eggplant, soups and stews, or a "durable" salad. "I am a peasant cook," she says, "but it must have eye appeal."

She likes to give "pitch-in parties," asking friends to each bring a dish to accompany a barbecue of chicken breasts, fish, or turkey. Pasta primavera and a "glorioso turkey burger" are other specialties, all reflecting a menu pattern keyed to low cholesterol. Fruit, granita, or a little cookie serves as dessert.

Lila relies on her own "whimsical garden" for much of the fare. Vegetables do best in raised beds, she finds; hers are made with surplus barrels and grape stakes with metal hoops.

A warm family spirit pervades at the Jaeger home, as children return with spouses and babies to romp on the lawn and picnic beside the pool.

MENU

ELEGANT ARTICHOKES*
RUTHERFORD HILL SAUVIGNON BLANC

•

UNCLE RAYMOND'S SAN FRANCISCO
BAY CIOPPINO*
CRISP SOURDOUGH FRENCH BREAD
DRIZZLED WITH OLIVE OIL
RUTHERFORD HILL ZINFANDEL

•

BROWNIES
RASPBERRIES WITH CRÈME FRAÎCHE
RUTHERFORD HILL MERLOT

Elegant Artichokes

8 medium-size artichokes
2 lemons
1½ quarts chicken stock
2 cloves garlic
¼ pound plus 1 tablespoon unsalted butter
1 cup freshly grated Parmesan cheese
About 2 cups Sauvignon Blanc or other dry white wine
1 shallot or green onion, chopped
¼ cup chopped fresh parsley

Remove a few of the outer leaves of each artichoke. With a stainless-steel knife, cut the stem ends flush with the bottoms and then cut about 1 inch off the tops. To prevent the artichokes from darkening, place them immediately in a large bowl of water to which the juice of one lemon has been added.

In a large pot, bring stock to a boil. Cut each artichoke in half lengthwise and place in the stock along with the garlic cloves. Boil gently for about 15 minutes or until just barely tender. Drain the artichokes and let cool slightly. With a spoon, scoop the prickly chokes from the centers.

Melt ¼ pound butter in a small pan and remove from the heat; place the cheese in a shallow bowl. Roll each artichoke half first in the melted butter and then in the cheese. Arrange the artichokes in a large ovenproof casserole and add wine to a depth of about ½ inch. Bake uncovered in a preheated 375° F. oven for 20 minutes, or until heated through, basting once or twice with the wine. If artichokes begin to dry out, add more wine as needed to keep them moist.

Just before serving, melt the remaining 1 tablespoon butter in a small skillet, add the shallot and parsley, and sauté for 1 minute. Squeeze in the juice of the remaining lemon and drizzle the mixture over the artichokes. Makes 8 servings.

Uncle Raymond's San Francisco Bay Cioppino

2 medium-size onions, chopped
3 cloves garlic, chopped
¼ cup olive oil
1 green bell pepper, seeded and chopped
1 stalk celery, chopped
1 large can (28 ounces) chopped Italian plum tomatoes, with liquid
2 cups dry red wine, preferably Cabernet Sauvignon or Zinfandel
1 teaspoon curry powder
1 teaspoon dried basil, crumbled
1 bay leaf
1 tablespoon minced fresh parsley
2 cans (6 ounces each) minced clams, with liquid
2 cups bottled clam juice
Salt and freshly ground black pepper to taste
¾ pound medium-size shrimp, peeled and deveined
¾ pound scallops, cut in half if large
1 pound firm white fish fillets, such as halibut, sea bass, rock cod, or snapper, cut into bite-size pieces

In a large kettle, sauté onions and garlic in oil until transparent, about 5 minutes. Add bell pepper and celery and sauté a few minutes longer. Add the tomatoes with liquid, 1 cup of the wine, curry powder, basil, bay leaf, and parsley. Cover and simmer 2 hours. Add clams with liquid, clam juice, and remaining 1 cup wine and season with salt and pepper. If desired, prepare up to this point in the morning of the day of serving or up to 24 hours in advance and refrigerate.

Just before serving, reheat, if made ahead, and add shrimp, scallops, and fish. Simmer gently for 8 to 10 minutes, then ladle into large soup bowls. Accompany with crisp sourdough French bread, brushed with extra-virgin olive oil, for dunking into the soup. Makes 8 servings.

MENU

PROSCIUTTO AND CRENSHAW SLICES
RUTHERFORD HILL SAUVIGNON BLANC

•

LILA'S SLICED BEEF TONGUE
WITH WINE-CAPER SAUCE*
BABY NEW POTATOES TOSSED WITH
CHIVES AND OLIVE OIL
SLICED TOMATOES WITH BASIL
ZUCCHINI SUMMER SALAD*
CRUSTY FRENCH ROLLS
RUTHERFORD HILL CHARDONNAY
JAEGER VINEYARD

•

CALIFORNIA CHÈVRE
BARTLETT PEARS WITH RED AND
GREEN SEEDLESS GRAPES
RUTHERFORD HILL CABERNET
SAUVIGNON OR MERLOT

Lila's Sliced Beef Tongue with Wine-Caper Sauce

1 fresh or corned beef tongue (about 3 pounds)
2 onions, each stuck with 2 whole cloves
1 large carrot, cut into chunks
3 stalks celery, cut into chunks
2 or 3 parsley sprigs
8 black peppercorns
2 cups Chardonnay or other dry white wine
2 tablespoons each butter and all-purpose flour
1 teaspoon dry mustard
½ cup whipping cream
1 egg yolk
1 tablespoon each balsamic vinegar and tarragon wine vinegar
3 tablespoons capers, drained, or to taste
Parsley sprigs for garnish

Place tongue in a large kettle with onions, carrot, celery, parsley sprigs, and peppercorns. Add the wine and enough hot water to cover barely. Bring to a boil and skim off any foam that forms on top. Lower the heat, cover, and simmer about 3 hours, or until the tongue is tender. Skim foam from liquid from time to time during cooking. Lift out tongue and let cool until it can be handled, then remove and discard skin and cut away any gristle or fat. Strain cooking liquid and return to kettle. Boil to reduce to 2 cups.

For the sauce, melt the butter in a saucepan placed over medium heat. Stir in the flour and mustard and cook, stirring, 2 to 3 minutes. Add the reduced stock and the cream, stirring constantly. In a mixing bowl, beat egg yolk with balsamic and tarragon vinegars and whisk in some of the hot sauce; stir yolk mixture into remaining sauce and cook, stirring, until thickened, about 5 minutes. Stir in capers and keep sauce warm.

To serve, cut tongue into ⅛-inch-thick slices, wrap in aluminum foil, and reheat in a preheated 375° F. oven for 15 minutes. Arrange tongue slices on a platter and spoon hot sauce over the top. Garnish with parsley sprigs. Makes 8 servings.

Zucchini Summer Salad

3 medium-size zucchini, cut into julienne
Seasoning salt
Vinaigrette (recipe follows)
1 red bell pepper, cut into julienne
1 yellow bell pepper, cut into julienne
3 green onions, including tops, chopped
½ cup coarsely chopped fresh parsley
1 large overgrown zucchini (optional)
Zucchini blossoms for garnish (optional)

Sprinkle julienned zucchini with seasoning salt, wrap in paper towels, and refrigerate for 30 minutes. Prepare the Vinaigrette.

Squeeze excess moisture from zucchini, pat dry, and place in a bowl with peppers, onions, and parsley. Stir in dressing and refrigerate at least 30 minutes, or for up to a few hours.

If you can find a very large zucchini, cut it lengthwise, making one-half slightly larger than the other. Hollow out the larger half, leaving a ¼-inch shell. Reserve the removed pulp and other half for another use. Spoon the salad mixture into the zucchini "boat" and garnish with a few zucchini blossoms. Alternatively, serve the salad in an attractive bowl. Makes 8 servings.

Vinaigrette In a jar with a tight-fitting lid, combine ⅓ cup vegetable oil, ⅓ cup olive oil, ¼ cup fresh lemon juice, and chopped fresh oregano, salt, and freshly ground black pepper to taste. Twist lid onto jar and shake well.

GRGICH HILLS CELLARS

A beret, a winning smile, and prize Chardonnays are trademarks of Miljenko (Mike) Grgich, winemaker and owner of Grgich Hills Cellar. Suntanned and with sparkling dark-brown eyes, Mike exudes a keen sense of humor and a merry mood as he pours a glass of wine and talks about his life.

He is one of eleven children, raised in Croatia, today a republic of Yugoslavia, where his father owned vineyards. "I remember stomping grapes when I was three years old," he says. "I have done my apprenticeship."

At the University of Zagreb he studied oenology and viniculture. Pressed by politics, he left the turmoil of Yugoslavia for the vineyards of California in 1958.

Before opening his own winery, Mike worked for several others, including Souverain, Beaulieu Vineyards, Christian Brothers, Robert Mondavi, and Château Montelena. It was the Chardonnay that he shaped for Montelena that stunned the French in a Paris blind tasting May 24, 1976, and helped thrust California wines into the world spotlight.

Mike concentrates on his celebrated Chardonnays. "If something works good for you, why change?" he asks. This varietal totals 50 percent of the seventeen thousand cases he produces in a year.

He also bottles Johannisberg Riesling, Zinfandel, and Fumé Blanc and recently made his first Cabernet Sauvignon. "I want to be known as the house of Chardonnay," he says, "but not all people prefer Chardonnay. I wish I could make only one wine, but I need to have more wines available."

"I'm not calling myself a wine maker any more," he continues. "I'm a wine sitter. I sit with the wine and see what it needs. Maturing of the wine is very important. Every point—the best grapes, the best equipment, the best people, the best care—I'm trying to do every point the best." Gold medals at wine expositions and first places in private tastings attest to his success.

Mike comes to work seven days a week and is usually the first one there, unlocking the chain across the driveway and turning on the irrigations system if the weather warrants. "I can come in on Saturday and Sunday and nobody chases me out. That's the bonus of ownership," he adds, smiling.

His wife, Tatjana, is also from Croatia and indulges him in his favorite Eastern European dishes. Their twenty-year-old daughter, Violet, is a music major at the University of California, Davis and is interested in wine. "I hope one day she will become a wine maker and take over when I crumble down," he says.

Swirling the wine, he observes, "I think America is great and California the best." And the beret? "It's my trademark, my small umbrella. I keep it on or in my pocket, handy all the time."

MENU

MUSHROOMS SAUTÉED WITH GARLIC*
GRGICH HILLS CHARDONNAY

•

DALMATIAN POT ROAST*
BAKED POTATOES
GRGICH HILLS CABERNET SAUVIGNON

•

BUTTER LETTUCE SALAD'
WITH VINAIGRETTE
BAVARIAN BLUE CHEESE

•

PARADIZET (FLOATING ISLAND)*

Mushrooms Sautéed with Garlic

¾ pound fresh button mushrooms (about 1 inch in diameter), fresh shiitake mushrooms, or small fresh oyster mushrooms, or a combination
3 tablespoons butter
3 cloves garlic, finely minced
1 teaspoon dried tarragon, crumbled
3 tablespoons chopped fresh parsley
Chive blossoms for garnish (optional)

Slice the button mushrooms. If using shiitake mushrooms, pull off stems; chop the stems and slice the caps. If using oyster mushrooms, leave whole. In a large skillet placed over medium heat, melt the butter, add mushrooms and garlic, and sauté quickly, stirring until mushrooms are glazed and just tender. Sprinkle with tarragon and parsley. Serve on individual plates. Garnish with chive blossoms, if desired. Makes 8 servings.

Dalmatian Pot Roast

1 boneless beef roast, such as rump (3 to 4 pounds)
4 cloves garlic, slivered
1 slice bacon, cut into ¼-inch dice
1 cup red-wine vinegar
4 whole cloves
2 tablespoons lard or vegetable oil
1 medium-size onion, grated
½ cup dry red wine
1½ cups beef stock
1 teaspoon granulated sugar
1 teaspoon tomato paste
¼ teaspoon freshly grated nutmeg
½ teaspoon freshly ground black pepper
1 medium-size celery root, peeled and coarsely chopped

With a knife tip, make 1-inch-deep slits over the surface of the roast and insert garlic slivers and bacon pieces into the slits. Place roast in a bowl, pour vinegar over it, add cloves, cover, and refrigerate for 2 days, turning occasionally.

Remove meat from marinade and pat dry. In a dutch oven, melt the lard and brown the roast, turning to sear all sides. Add onion and sauté a few minutes. Add wine, stock, sugar, tomato paste, and nutmeg, cover, and simmer for 1½ hours. Add celery root and simmer for 15 minutes or until meat is tender. Slice roast and serve with vegetables and pan juices alongside. Makes 8 to 10 servings.

Paradizet (Floating Island)

4 eggs, separated
⅛ teaspoon salt
¾ cup granulated sugar
3 cups milk
2 egg yolks
1 teaspoon vanilla extract
⅓ cup grated semi-sweet chocolate

In a mixing bowl, beat egg whites with salt until frothy. Gradually adding ¼ cup sugar, beat until soft peaks form. Heat milk to simmering in a large skillet. Dip a serving spoon into cold water and then scoop up about one-eighth of the whites. Drop the spoonful of whites into the simmering milk. Repeat with remaining whites, dipping the spoon into cold water before forming each spoonful. Poach the 8 meringues for 2 to 3 minutes, turning them once with a spoon dipped in hot water. (If necessary, cook the meringues in 2 batches to avoid crowding them in the skillet.) With a slotted spoon, transfer the meringues to a plate rinsed with cold water and let cool. Reserve the hot milk to make the custard.

Prepare a stirred custard. Beat the 6 egg yolks until light and beat in remaining ½ cup sugar. Pour hot milk into the yolk mixture and turn into the top pan of a double boiler placed over simmering water. Cook, stirring, until custard coats a spoon, about 10 minutes. Remove from the heat and stir in vanilla extract. Cool, cover, and refrigerate. To serve, spoon custard into dessert bowls and float meringues on top. Sprinkle with chocolate. Makes 8 servings.

MENU

WINE CONSOMMÉ
CHEESE STICKS
GRGICH SAUVIGNON BLANC

•

SOLE FILLET ROLLS IN WINE SAUCE*
STEAMED ASPARAGUS
NEW POTATOES
WITH WATERCRESS BUTTER
GRGICH CHARDONNAY

•

STRAWBERRIES
WITH RASPBERRY SAUCE
AND WHIPPED CREAM

Sole Fillet Rolls in Wine Sauce

8 sole fillets (about 5 ounces each)
1 cup Sauvignon Blanc or other dry white wine
½ cup water
2 bay leaves
2 cloves garlic, chopped
½ teaspoon dried rosemary, crumbled
2 slices onion
1 slice lemon
¼ teaspoon each salt and white pepper
4 slices bacon, blanched 30 seconds and halved lengthwise
2 egg yolks
½ cup whipping cream
1 tablespoon butter
2 lemons, sliced, for garnish

Roll up fish fillets and secure with a toothpick. In a large skillet, combine the wine, water, bay leaves, garlic, rosemary, onion, lemon slice, salt, and pepper and bring to a boil. Lower the heat and simmer for 5 minutes. Add fish rolls and poach, covered, for 4 to 5 minutes, or until barely cooked through. With a slotted spoon, remove to a platter; reserve stock. Wrap each fish fillet with a strip of bacon and secure with another toothpick. Slip under the broiler just to crisp bacon slightly, about 2 minutes; remove to a platter and keep warm.

Strain fish stock, pour into a saucepan, and boil to reduce to ¾ cup. Beat egg yolks until light and whisk in cream. Whisk a little of the hot stock into the yolk mixture, then pour the yolk mixture into the saucepan, whisking constantly. Cook over medium heat, stirring, until thickened. Swirl in butter. Remove toothpicks from fish rolls and spoon sauce over the rolls. Garnish with lemon slices. Makes 8 servings.

MATANZAS
CREEK
WINERY

1984

SONOMA COUNTY
CHARDONNAY

A TABLE WINE PRODUCED AND BOTTLED BY
MATANZAS CREEK WINERY, SANTA ROSA, CALIF., BW-CA-4848.

MATANZAS CREEK WINERY

"Creole cooking is the food I love best," says vivacious Sandra MacIver, president and owner of Matanzas Creek Winery. "It is better the second day and great for entertaining. Made ahead, it allows you to serve a lot of people with little help. Sometimes we pull in Texas fare, as Bill is from Texas. His chili, made without beans, is a big hit."

Fajitas are another family favorite. Skirt steak is marinated in lime juice and garlic, then grilled, cut across the grain, and served on warm tortillas with chopped onions, diced tomatoes, and sour cream. This dish "garnered a standing ovation from the Mexican pickers at a crew dinner," Sandra announces proudly. "They said it was better than in a Mexican restaurant."

The MacIvers' new winery is nestled in the oak-tree-covered hillside of Bennet Mountain, affording a panoramic view of vineyards, ponds, and pastureland, as well as the Sonoma Valley. The modern two-story structure makes a strong statement for food and wine. A spacious, open kitchen joins the reception area, just off the combined conference and dining room.

When the crowd is too large for these rooms, a party is staged in the barrel and tank rooms. "I try to put my money in the food and let the ambience be natural, yet festive,"

explains Sandra. That means utilizing grape-picking baskets to hold pots of flowering pink, red, and yellow celosia, or papering the walls with blown-up posters and letting helium-filled balloons billow aloft.

Two teenage daughters keep the family aimed toward a healthful, informal dining style. "I like to do lots of grilling, as we try to avoid all fats in our diet, " explains Sandra. "We may grill potatoes and Japanese eggplants until they almost caramelize, to go with a California menu."

Sandra grew up in New Orleans in a formal home with servants. She majored in art at Mills College in Oakland, California, and has used her early training to create the wine labels and to design printed materials and visual displays.

In the early seventies her interest in wine and a desire to raise her children in a rural environment prompted her to settle in Bennett Valley. The new home was a former dairy ranch with two hundred acres of grazing land and wooded hillsides.

One of Sandra's first projects was putting in vineyards. She rebuilt the old dairy barn into a building for the winery's first crush in 1978. As her vineyards grew, so did demand for Matanzas Creek's award-winning wines. In 1985 the new facility was completed.

Sandra and Bill were married in 1980. Bill served in the United States Air Force for twenty-one years and upon retirement earned a master's degree in psychology. He was in private practive when Sandra introduced him to the wine business. Now he serves as vice-president and general manager. "We work as a team. It is too hard to do it by oneself," says Sandra.

"Bill also cooks. The day I decided to marry him he was making *paella*."

The couple is active in trade and community boards. Sandra has the distinction of being the first woman to serve as president of the board of directors of the Sonoma County Winegrowers Association.

MENU

BEGGARS' PURSES*
BELGIAN ENDIVE, CHÈVRE,
AND BAY SHRIMP*
MATANZAS CREEK
SONOMA COUNTY SAUVIGNON BLANC

•

GRILLED POUSSINS
WITH ZUCCHINI-CHEESE STUFFING*
GRILLED POTATO SPEARS,
JAPANESE EGGPLANTS,
AND CHERRY TOMATOES*
MATANZAS CREEK
SONOMA COUNTY CHARDONNAY

•

BASKET OF CHERRIES,
APRICOTS, AND GRAPES
SPARKLING CHARDONNAY

Beggars' Purses

Crêpes (recipe follows)
1 cup sour cream
⅓ cup golden caviar
16 green onion tops, blanched

Prepare Crêpes in advance. Just before serving, heat sour cream in the top pan of a double boiler placed over simmering water. Working quickly, assemble purses by spooning a dollop of sour cream and a spoonful of caviar onto the center of each crêpe. Gather each crêpe into a bundle, the shape of a drawstring purse, and tie with a green onion leaf. Serve immediately. Makes about 16 appetizers.

Crêpes Combine 1 cup milk, 3 eggs, and ⅓ cup all-purpose flour in a blender or a food processor fitted with a metal blade and blend until smooth. Heat a 6- or 7-inch crêpe pan over medium heat, add ½ teaspoon butter, and tilt pan to coat surface evenly with melted butter. Pour in just enough batter to coat surface (less than 2 tablespoons) and quickly tilt pan to cover surface. Cook crêpe until golden brown on the edges and dry on top. Turn out onto a plate. Repeat with remaining batter, adding more butter to pan as needed. Stack crêpes (there should be about 16 in all), wrap in foil, and refrigerate 1 to 2 days. To reheat, bring crêpes to room temperature without opening foil. Place foil packet in a preheated 325° F. oven for 6 to 8 minutes.

Belgian Endive, Chèvre, and Bay Shrimp

2 heads Belgian endive
4 ounces California chèvre fromage blanc, at room temperature
4 ounces bay shrimp

Separate endive into individual leaves. Put the fromage blanc into a pastry bag fitted with a star point and pipe a bite-size amount of the cheese onto the base of each endive leaf. Drop 3 to 4 shrimp onto the cheese. Arrange filled leaves on a platter and serve at room temperature. Makes about 16 appetizers.

Grilled Poussins with Zucchini-Cheese Stuffing

1 pound zucchini
5 tablespoons unsalted butter, at room temperature
1 medium-size onion, finely chopped
3 ounces cream cheese, at room temperature
1 egg
½ teaspoon dried thyme, crumbled
½ cup freshly grated Parmesan cheese
8 poussins
Olive oil
Fines herbes

Grate zucchini, sprinkle with salt, wrap in paper towels, and let stand 15 minutes for juices to exude. Squeeze zucchini dry. In a skillet placed over medium heat, melt 1 tablespoon butter, add zucchini, and sauté until crisp-tender; remove from the skillet and let cool. In the same skillet, melt 1 tablespoon butter, add onion, and sauté until transparent, about 5 minutes; remove from the heat and let cool. In a bowl, beat together cream cheese and remaining 3 tablespoons butter until blended. Add egg and beat until smooth. Mix in sautéed onion, sautéed zucchini, thyme, and Parmesan cheese.

Using your fingers, loosen the skin from the breast of each poussin, working from the body cavity opening. Force a small amount of the zucchini stuffing between the skin and breast. Truss birds. Rub poussins with oil and then with a light coating of fines herbes. Arrange poussins over a medium-hot mesquite fire in a covered grill and roast for about 20 minutes, or until done to your liking. Remove to a platter and let rest a few minutes before serving. Makes 8 servings.

Grilled Potato Spears, Japanese Eggplants, and Cherry Tomatoes

3 large baking
   potatoes
Olive oil
Salt and freshly
   ground black
   pepper to taste
4 small Japanese
   eggplants
2 cups cherry
   tomatoes (about
   ½ pound)

Wash the potatoes, but do not peel. Cut each potato lengthwise into 8 wedges. Toss in oil to coat lightly and then season with salt and pepper. Cut off ends of unpeeled eggplants and slice in half lengthwise. Coat with oil and season with salt and pepper as you did potatoes. Season the whole cherry tomatoes in the same manner.

Arrange vegetables on grill with poussins, putting the potatoes near the center of the grill and the eggplants around the edges. Cook in the covered grill for about 20 to 25 minutes, checking frequently and turning as needed. Add tomatoes at the last minute and cook only a few seconds. Makes 8 servings.

MENU

CATFISH MORSELS*
MATANZAS CREEK
SONOMA COUNTY SAUVIGNON BLANC
•
OYSTERS ROCKEFELLER
MATANZAS CREEK ESTATE BOTTLED
SONOMA VALLEY CHARDONNAY
•
SHRIMP CREOLE*
STEAMED WHITE RICE
GREEN SALAD WITH VINAIGRETTE
BAGUETTES WITH SWEET BUTTER
MATANZAS CREEK
SONOMA VALLEY MERLOT
•
CAFÉ BRÛLOT*

Catfish Morsels

2 pounds catfish fillets
Salt and freshly
   ground black
   pepper to taste
Tabasco sauce to taste
   or Blackened
   Redfish Seasoning
2 eggs, lightly beaten
Yellow cornmeal
Peanut oil for frying

Season catfish fillets with salt, pepper, and Tabasco and let stand for 30 minutes. Cut fillets into bite-size pieces, dip pieces in beaten egg, and dredge in cornmeal. Heat the oil to 375° F., or until a bit of bread sizzles and browns within seconds of being dropped into the hot oil. Drop in some catfish pieces, being careful not to crowd the pan, and cook for 2 minutes, or until crispy. Lift out with a slotted utensil and drain on paper towels; keep them warm while cooking the remaining fish. Makes about 12 servings.

Shrimp Creole

Shrimp Stock (recipe
   follows)
¼ cup vegetable oil or
   rendered bacon fat
3 medium-size yellow
   onions, chopped
½ cup chopped green
   onions
2 green bell peppers,
   seeded and coarsely
   chopped
2 cloves garlilc,
   minced
2 stalks celery with
   leaves, chopped
1 teaspoon dried
   thyme, crumbled
2 bay leaves
¼ cup all-purpose
   flour
1 can (16 ounces)
   tomatoes, coarsely
   chopped, with
   liquid
1 can (8 ounces)
   tomato sauce
Salt and freshly
   ground black
   pepper to taste
4 pounds medium-size
   shrimp, peeled and
   deveined
1 to 2 teaspoons
   Tabasco sauce, or
   to taste
3 tablespoons minced
   fresh parsley

Prepare the Shrimp Stock. In a large pot placed over medium heat, heat oil or bacon fat, add yellow onions, green onions, bell peppers, garlic, celery, thyme, and bay leaves, and sauté until onions are transparent, about 5 minutes. Add flour and cook a few minutes. Add tomatoes, tomato sauce, 2 cups Shrimp Stock, salt, and pepper and simmer, partially covered, 1 hour.

Remove bay leaves from pot and add shrimp. Cook just until shrimp turn pink, about 3 to 5 minutes. Season with Tabasco and sprinkle with parsley. Serve over hot cooked rice. Makes 12 servings.

Shrimp Stock In a large saucepan, combine shrimp heads and shells reserved from cleaning shrimp for recipe, 1 medium-size onion, cut into quarters, 1 stalk celery, cut into pieces, 1 bay leaf, and 3 cups water. Bring to a boil, cover partially, lower the heat, and simmer for 30 minutes. Strain, pressing shells against strainer to release as much flavor as possible. There should be about 2 cups stock.

Café Brûlot

Peel of 1 orange
   (without any white
   membrane), thinly
   sliced
3 2-inch cinnamon
   sticks
10 whole cloves
1½ tablespoons
   granulated sugar
6 ounces Cognac
4 cups hot strong
   black coffee

In a flameproof bowl or chafing dish, combine the orange peel, cinnamon sticks, cloves, sugar, and Cognac and heat over a chafing dish burner or on the range over medium heat. When Cognac is hot but not boiling, scoop out a small ladleful, ignite it, and then stir it as it flames into the mixture remaining in the bowl. Pour the hot coffee into the Cognac mixture and ladle into demitasses or brûlot cups. Makes 12 servings.

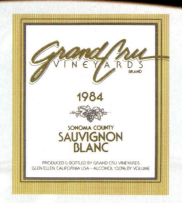

Grand Cru
VINEYARDS
BRAND

1984

SONOMA COUNTY
SAUVIGNON
BLANC

PRODUCED & BOTTLED BY GRAND CRU VINEYARDS
GLEN ELLEN, CALIFORNIA USA — ALCOHOL 13.0% BY VOLUME

GRAND CRU VINEYARDS

To keep earning his daily bread peddling bread, Walt Dreyer was told "move east." Instead he bought a winery, forgoing the ladder to corporate success.

Walt had worked for twenty-five years for the San Francisco–based baking business founded by his father. When the company expanded nationwide and then was sold to Continental Grain, he and his wife, Tina, began to think of alternatives, of something they could do together. Both had degrees from Stanford University, he in geology and she in psychology.

In 1978 they started looking at wineries. After seeing about two hundred properties, they found Grand Cru. "It was a marvelous facility, a jewel, had a good reputation and its obvious need was management," says Tina. "It fit what we needed."

Walt chose to leave his executive position "with all the perks" and they bought Grand Cru in 1980. "The whole family, including our three teenage sons, knuckled down," observes Tina. "It's been a great experience for them, to become more responsible and not have everything handed to them."

Grand Cru was founded a century ago on thirty-five acres of vineyards in Sonoma. Since the Dreyers' purchase, the operation has made a dramatic turn-around. Production has expanded

fivefold, to fifty thousand cases annually. Today the winery turns out five varietals, with emphasis on fruity white wines.

Sons Dan, Matt, and John all work at the winery during school breaks. Walt is the full-time manager and directs sales. Tina helps market the wine nationwide, produces a newsletter, and entertains.

She is an award-winning cook who especially loves to bake—breads, cakes, and pastries. "My own personal challenge is always to try something new," explains Tina. "I aim to learn a cooking technique so it becomes second nature."

At their spacious Spanish-style contemporary home in Woodside, California, she works in a large open kitchen that adjoins a family sitting-and-dining area and opens to a garden patio surrounded by home vineyards. The kitchen is equipped with hanging copper pans and the latest appliances, including a gelato machine. She uses the latter to make sorbets, even a pomegranate-flavored one, from the abundant fruit of family orchards.

Walt's family grows grapes, pears, citrus, pomegranates, olives, cotton, and tomatoes on several southern California ranches and Tina cultivates an expansive vegetable and herb garden and vineyard on their acreage at home.

Because the winery lacks a kitchen, the entertaining there centers around picnics and barbecues. A typical party is twelve to eighteen guests for a luncheon. Tina likes to feature foods of Sonoma County, which means, among other things, sausages, French bread, and Jack cheese. The meals are hearty and typically include her homemade braided Gruyère cheese bread. For dessert she tries a different cake every time, perhaps a Port-laced chocolate or a hazelnut cake with orange liqueur.

MENU

SCALLOPS AND AVOCADO
WITH RED PEPPER SAUCE*
CHEESE BRAID*
GRAND CRU SAUVIGNON BLANC
•
BUTTERFLIED LEG OF LAMB
IN POMEGRANATE JUICE*
GRILLED VEGETABLES*
SAUTÉED CORN*
GRAND CRU CABERNET SAUVIGNON
•
MOUSSE GRAND CRU*
GRAND CRU
LATE HARVEST GEWÜRZTRAMINER

Scallops and Avocado with Red Pepper Sauce

1½ pounds scallops, halved if large

Fresh lime or lemon juice

Red Pepper Sauce (see Basic Recipes)

3 avocados

Marinate scallops in lime juice until opaque, about 3 hours. Prepare the Red Pepper Sauce.

To serve, place a pool of sauce on each salad plate. Peel, pit, and slice the avocados and arrange with scallops in an attractive pattern on the sauce. Makes 8 servings.

Cheese Braid

1 package active dry yeast (scant 1 tablespoon)

1 cup lukewarm water (about 110°F.)

3½ cups unbleached bread flour

1 tablespoon granulated sugar

1 teaspoon salt

12 tablespoons (¾ cup) butter, at room temperature and cut into small pieces

4 eggs, at room temperature

1½ cups (6 ounces) shredded Gruyère cheese

Glaze of 1 egg, beaten with 1 tablespoon milk

In a mixing bowl, sprinkle yeast into warm water and let stand until dissolved and foamy, about 10 minutes. Add 1½ cups flour, sugar, and salt to yeast and beat with a wooden spoon or an electric mixer for 2 minutes. Beat butter pieces into flour mixture until incorporated. Mix in eggs, one at a time, then beat in remaining 2 cups flour, ½ cup at a time. Beat dough until smooth, satiny, and elastic, about 10 minutes. Dough will be soft. Stir in cheese. Cover bowl and let dough rise in a warm place until doubled in volume, about 1½ hours. Punch down and refrigerate overnight, or at least several hours.

To shape, knead cold dough on a lightly floured board to soften slightly. Divide into 3 equal portions and roll each portion into a rope about 18 inches long. Place the 3 ropes parallel on a greased baking sheet, then form them into a braid, pinching the ends together. Cover and let rise in a warm place until doubled in volume. Brush with glaze and bake in a preheated 400° F. oven for 30 minutes, or until loaf is golden and sounds hollow when thumped. Let cool 1 or 2 minutes, then slide onto wire rack to cool. Makes 1 loaf.

Butterflied Leg of Lamb in Pomegranate Juice

4 cloves garlic

1 leg of lamb (4 to 5 pounds), boned and butterflied

1 cup pomegranate juice

½ teaspoon freshly ground black pepper

3 tablespoons chopped fresh rosemary, or 2 teaspoons dried rosemary, crumbled

Peel the garlic and cut into slivers. With a knife tip, make shallow slashes in the lamb and insert the garlic slivers into the meat. Marinate meat overnight in a mixture of pomegranate juice, pepper, and rosemary. Remove meat from marinade and grill over a hot charcoal fire, basting frequently with the marinade and grilling on both sides until still pink inside, about 15 to 20 minutes. Slice into strips to serve. Makes 8 servings.

Grilled Vegetables

4 medium-size zucchini, halved lengthwise

4 small Japanese eggplants, halved lengthwise

Salt

8 slices onion (½ inch thick)

¼ cup olive oil

2 tablespoons red-wine vinegar

Olive oil for basting

2 tablespoons chopped fresh thyme, or 1½ teaspoons dried thyme, crumbled

Freshly ground black pepper to taste

Sprinkle zucchini halves and eggplant halves with salt. Wrap in paper towels for 30 minutes. At the same time, marinate onion slices in olive oil and vinegar for 30 minutes. Pat zucchini and eggplants dry and place on a grill over a slow charcoal fire. Baste vegetables with olive oil and cook only until they are light brown and soft, about 15 minutes. Simultaneously, remove onion slices from marinade, reserving marinade, and grill over a slow fire until soft, about 15 minutes.

Remove all the vegetables from the grill and season the onion slices with some of the reserved marinade, thyme, salt, and pepper. Sprinkle the eggplant and zucchini with thyme. Makes 8 servings.

Sautéed Corn
8 large ears of corn
¼ pound (½ cup) unsalted butter
½ cup whipping cream or milk
Salt and freshly ground black pepper to taste

With a sharp knife, scrape the kernels from the corn. In a skillet, melt the butter, add corn, and stir over low heat 1 minute. Add cream, season with salt and pepper, and cook only until corn is hot. Makes 8 servings.

Mousse Grand Cru
1¾ cups Gewürztraminer
¾ cup granulated sugar
2 packages (scant 1 tablespoon each) unflavored gelatin
½ cup cold water
1 can (20 ounces) lychees, drained
Juice of 1 lemon
2 cups whipping cream

Strawberries for garnish
Sabayon Sauce (see Basic Recipes)

In a saucepan, combine the wine and sugar, bring to a boil, lower the heat, and simmer for 10 minutes. Sprinkle gelatin over the cold water and let sit about 5 minutes to soften. Add wine mixture to gelatin and stir until dissolved. Purée lychees in a blender or a food processor fitted with a metal blade. (This will yield about ¾ cup purée.) Add purée and lemon juice to gelatin mixture. Cover and chill until syrupy. Whip cream until soft peaks form and fold into gelatin mixture. Pour into individual molds or a single 2-quart mold. Chill until set. Prepare the Sabayon Sauce.

To serve, dip molds into hot water to reach halfway up their sides for a few seconds, then invert onto serving plates. (In the case of a single mold, loosen mousse in the same manner, but invert onto a platter.) Garnish with strawberries and spoon Sabayon Sauce over the top. Makes 8 servings.

MENU
ASSORTED GRILLED SAUSAGES*
CHEESE BOARD
SONOMA FRENCH BREAD
PAPAYA AND AVOCADO SALAD*
CREAMY POTATO SALAD*
GRAND CRU CHENIN BLANC,
GEWÜRZTRAMINER,
CABERNET SAUVIGNON,
AND ZINFANDEL

•

CHOCOLATE CHIP OATMEAL COOKIES*

Assorted Grilled Sausages
3 to 4 pounds assorted sausages, such as bratwurst, mettwurst, garlic, and/or Polish
Chenin Blanc or other dry white wine

Place sausages on a grill over a medium-hot fire and cook, turning, until lightly browned, about 8 minutes. Transfer sausages to a large skillet, add wine to cover, bring to a simmer, and remove from the heat. Let stand, covered, for 15 minutes or longer until serving time. If desired, omit the grilling and instead sauté the sausages in a little butter until browned; then cover them with the wine, bring to a simmer, and remove from the heat. Makes 8 servings.

Papaya and Avocado Salad
2 papayas
2 avocados
½ cup walnut oil
3 tablespoons raspberry-wine vinegar
Salt and freshly ground black pepper to taste
½ cup chopped toasted walnuts

Peel papayas, halve, and remove seeds. Peel avocados, halve, and remove seeds. Cut the fruits lengthwise into ¼-inch-thick slices and transfer the sliced halves, in their original shapes, to a platter. Fan out the slices slightly. Mix together the oil, vinegar, salt, and pepper and drizzle over the fruit. Sprinkle with nuts. Makes 8 servings.

Creamy Potato Salad
3 pounds small red new potatoes
½ cup chopped green onions
½ cup chopped fresh parsley
2 teaspoons chopped fresh tarragon
⅔ cup mayonnaise (preferably homemade)
½ cup sour cream or crème fraîche
Salt and white pepper to taste

Scrub potatoes and steam or boil for 10 to 12 minutes, or until tender but still firm. Drain and chill. Cut smaller potatoes in half, or larger ones in 1-inch pieces. Place potatoes in a bowl and add onions, parsley, tarragon, mayonnaise, sour cream, salt, and pepper. Mix lightly. Cover and chill overnight. Makes 8 servings.

Chocolate Chip Oatmeal Cookies
½ pound (1 cup) butter
1½ cups firmly packed brown sugar
½ cup granulated sugar
2 eggs
1 teaspoon vanilla extract
½ teaspoon salt
1 teaspoon baking soda
2 cups all-purpose flour
1 cup coarsely ground walnuts or pecans
1 cup quick-cooking oatmeal
1 package (6 ounces) semisweet chocolate chips

In a mixing bowl, cream butter until light and fluffy. Add sugars and beat until smooth. Add eggs and vanilla, mixing well. Stir together salt, soda, and flour and add to butter mixture, beating just until blended. Stir in nuts, oatmeal, and chocolate chips. Drop by tablespoonfuls onto greased baking sheets, placing 2 inches apart. Flatten slightly. Bake in a preheated 350° F. oven for 10 minutes, or until golden brown. Makes about 3½ dozen.

STAG'S LEAP WINE CELLARS

The handcrafted wines of Stag's Leap Wine Cellars were a well-kept California secret until they gained international fame at a 1976 Paris tasting. The winery's first vintage, a Stag's Leap 1973 Cabernet Sauvignon, took top honors in direct competition with France's finest Bordeaux and the best Cabernets of California.

Since then, Warren Winiarski, proprietor, general manager, and wine maker, has been racking up honors both for the winery and the Napa Valley, with vintages characterized by varietal excellence, elegance, restraint, and balance.

A scholar turned vintner, Warren pursued an academic career, teaching political theory at the University of Chicago until 1964, when he came to the Napa Valley. He apprenticed in turn with two of California's master wine makers, Lee Stewart and Robert Mondavi.

Warren's plan was to have his own vineyard. He supervised the planting of Stag's Leap Vineyards in 1970, and in 1972, with wife Barbara as general partner, founded the winery on an oak-dotted knoll off Napa's Silverado Trail.

Since then the reds have been two-time winners of the Harry Waugh Trophy at the International Wine and Spirits Competition in England and have won tastings similar to the Paris event. In 1983 two Stag's Leap wines were selected by Queen Elizabeth's Clerk of the Royal Cellar as the only California wines served at an anniversary dinner honoring President and Mrs. Reagan aboard Her Majesty's yacht *Britannia.*

It was actually Warren's interest in the Italian Renaissance, pursued while studying in Florence and Naples, that opened his eyes to wine. After returning to the United States, he stopped drinking wine for a few years. "But then a friend brought over a bottle to accompany dinner one night, and it was after that that I started to think about another life besides academics. There was a desire to involve the family as a unit; that couldn't be done in an academic life."

At the time, some kind of agriculture looked like a good vocation. "It became clear to me that to make it viable as a family enterprise, one couldn't simply grow apples," he recalls. "One had to get hold of the entire process. Grape growing and wine making seemed noble."

Barbara is an accomplished hostess and orchestrating food and wine events has become practically routine for her. On a summer weekend she may handle an elegant six-course dinner for two dozen, an intimate luncheon for eight, and an informal dinner with Greek dancing for fifty. The oak-umbrellaed garden patio makes a romantic outdoor setting in the twilight.

Eldest daughter Kasia is an adept culinary assistant and the marketing director for the firm. Two other children, Stephen and Julia, are pursuing careers away from the winery.

"The big thing in entertaining is to have the freshest and best of the season and keep it pretty," suggests Barbara. Over the years she has gained an understanding of the basic culinary processes and rarely relies on a cookbook. "That is the fun of cooking, to launch into one's own style," she says.

For Christmas Eve dinner, the family follows the Polish tradition of *Wigilia,* the vigil meal of seven, nine, or eleven courses at which no meat is served. "It is a 'fast' dinner that in fact becomes a feast," exclaims Barbara.

Melding their talents with food and wine, the Winiarskis set a splendid table, intertwining fresh California offerings with a range of ethnic cuisines.

MENU

COLD CUCUMBER SOUP*
STAG'S LEAP SAUVIGNON BLANC

•

GAME HENS IN A NEST*
STAG'S LEAP CHARDONNAY

•

CHÈVRE AND SUN-DRIED TOMATOES
STAG'S LEAP MERLOT

•

CABERNET CHERRIES STAG'S LEAP*

Cold Cucumber Soup
2 large cucumbers
3 cups chicken stock
¼ cup dry white wine
2 tablespoons white-wine vinegar
¼ teaspoon salt
⅛ teaspoon white pepper
1 tablespoon chopped fresh dill, or ¾ teaspoon dried dill, crumbled
2 tablespoons cornstarch, blended with 2 tablespoons cold water
½ cup each sour cream and plain yogurt
Plain yogurt and dill sprigs for garnish

Peel cucumbers and cut in half lengthwise. Remove the seeds with a spoon and then dice the cucumbers. Purée cucumbers and 1 cup stock in a blender or a food processor fitted with a metal blade. Place cucumber purée and remaining 2 cups stock in a large saucepan. Add wine, vinegar, salt, pepper, and dill. Bring to a boil, cover, lower the heat, and simmer 5 minutes. Blend ½ cup of the soup into the cornstarch mixture, return mixture to the saucepan, and cook, stirring, until soup thickens. Remove from the heat and let cool. Stir in sour cream and yogurt. Refrigerate 2 hours or longer. Ladle into bowls and garnish with yogurt and dill sprigs. Makes 6 servings.

Game Hens in a Nest
3 Cornish game hens
Olive oil
½ teaspoon dried tarragon or thyme
½ cup beef consommé
2 tablespoons Chardonnay
8 quail eggs, hard-cooked
1 basket (2 cups) alfalfa sprouts
Finely julienned carrots, green bell peppers, and celery

Rub game hens with oil and tarragon and place on a rack in a roasting pan. Roast in a preheated 425° F. oven for 30 to 35 minutes, or until leg joints move freely. Remove from the oven and let cool.

Cut hens in half and place cut side down on a large platter, arranging them in a ring with legs inward. Heat consommé with wine and brush onto the birds. Mound alfalfa sprouts in the center of the ring. Peel quail eggs and halve 1 or 2 for the "broken eggs." Place eggs on the sprout "nest." Around the hens, form a ring of "summer grasses" with the julienned carrots, peppers, and celery. Makes 6 servings.

Cabernet Cherries Stag's Leap
1 cup Cabernet Sauvignon
½ cup granulated sugar
1 2-inch cinnamon stick
Strip lemon peel
Dash brandy
1½ pounds Bing cherries, pitted (about 3 cups)
Crème fraîche or lightly whipped cream

In a large saucepan placed over medium heat, combine the wine, sugar, cinnamon stick, lemon peel, and brandy. Simmer for 20 minutes, remove from the heat, let cool, and strain. About 1 hour before serving, add the cherries to the spiced wine. Serve in dessert bowls, garnished with crème fraîche. Makes 6 servings.

MENU

PICKLED HERRING
INDIVIDUAL BEET, CARROT,
AND CELERY SALADS
CALIFORNIA SPARKLING WINE

•

WILD MUSHROOM SOUP
STAG'S LEAP SAUVIGNON BLANC

•

BAKED SALMON WITH
LEEK TARRAGON BUTTER*
PARSLIED POTATOES
STAG'S LEAP CHARDONNAY

•

DRIED-FRUIT COMPOTE*
STAG'S LEAP LATE HARVEST RIESLING

•

POPPY-SEED PASTRY, NUTS,
CHOCOLATES

Baked Salmon with Leek Tarragon Butter*

Olive oil
⅓ cup chopped
    shallots
Salt and freshly
    ground black
    pepper
1 whole salmon (4 to
    5 pounds)
Fresh dill branches
1 cup Sauvignon Blanc
    or other dry white
    wine
Leek Tarragon Butter
    (recipe follows)

Lay a large piece of heavy-duty foil in a shallow baking pan. The foil should be large enough to reach several inches beyond the sides of the pan. Coat bottom surface of foil generously with oil, top with chopped shallots, and season with salt and pepper. Arrange the fish on the foil so it curves, and thus appears to be swimming. Drape dill around its back and sides and tuck the cut ends under the belly. Crimp up foil sides to form a bowl shape and pour wine into the base of the "bowl." Bring foil sides together and completely encase fish in the foil, making a tightly sealed packet. Bake in a preheated 350° F. oven for 50 minutes, or until fish just barely flakes with a fork.

While fish cooks, prepare the Leek Butter Sauce. Open packet at the table and baste each salmon serving with foil juices. Accompany with leek sauce. Makes 8 or more servings.

Leek Butter Sauce

Mince 1 shallot and the white part only of 1 leek. Place in a small saucepan with 3 tablespoons each white-wine vinegar and dry white wine; boil until reduced to 2 tablespoons. Add 12 tablespoons (¾ cup) butter, 1 tablespoon at a time, heating over low heat and beating with a wire whisk until incorporated. Season with ½ teaspoon dried tarragon, crumbled, and salt and freshly ground pepper to taste.

Dried-Fruit Compote

1 pound mixed dried
    fruit, including
    prunes, pears,
    apricots, and
    apples in any
    proportion
About 2 cups water
½ cup granulated
    sugar
2 2-inch cinnamon
    sticks
3 strips lemon peel
2 tablespoons brandy

Soak fruit overnight in 2 cups water, or as needed to cover fruit. Place fruit and soaking water in a saucepan and add sugar, cinnamon sticks, and lemon peel. Bring to a low simmer and cook gently for 30 minutes, adding water if liquid begins to cook away. Remove from the heat, stir in brandy, and let cool. (If a thicker syrup is desired, pour off the cooking liquid and boil to reduce.) Serve compote at room temperature. Makes 8 servings.

CHAPPELLET VINEYARDS

Molly Chappellet is in her glory in the garden, filling a huge wicker basket with gorgeous, unusual vegetables. Unconsciously the arrangement becomes a striking still life, a stylized design that excites the eye in the same way a painting does. Peppers in all hues, scarlet Swiss chard, purple basil, and celadon squash intermix with ivory pumpkins, artichokes, and golden plum tomatoes.

Molly's talents encompass not only growing these gems, but also utilizing them in striking table decor and, of course, turning them into marvelous dishes. "My cooking has revolved around serving a crowd," she says. She and vintner husband Donn have raised six children on Pritchard Hill, an idyllic setting that overlooks Lake Hennesse, the Chappellet vineyards, and the expansive vegetable and berry garden.

They moved to the valley in 1968, when Donn left a successful food-vending business in southern California. Their three daughters and three sons are now launched in their own varied careers, yet they still return for family gatherings.

"I'm geared for numbers," says Molly, "and great at throwing things together at the last minute. I like to do things spontaneously." Donn is an accomplished cook as well, with breakfasts his forte.

Molly likes to put a surprise in their menus. Sometimes they have a "maize feast," dining only on fresh-picked corn. One year they planted eight varieties, had a corn tasting, and tallied the votes. Silver Queen won, and this year the stalks stood ten feet tall. She loves to pick the tiny, finger-size ears for eating raw or for garnishing a plate.

After years of doing table decorations for charity events and helping artist friends promote their works, Molly has launched her own business, Art Forms. Swift and skillful at creating arrangements, she thoroughly enjoys the challenge. She likes to style the decor to the mood and feeling of the occasion.

"With a winery you have to entertain a great deal," she observes. Today her table centerpieces are both eclectic and striking. A dinner guest may be confronted with an array of red peppers, a pyramid of bread loaves, or a pile of lemons in paint buckets.

Put simply, Molly Chappellet feels that table setting is an art; it is both an important contribution to the enjoyment of Chappellet wines and a distinctive backdrop to a meal.

MENU

FRESHLY SQUEEZED ORANGE JUICE
MIXED WITH CHAPPELLET RIESLING
APPLE RINGS* (IN WINTER)
FRESH SNOW PEACHES OR BERRIES
(IN SUMMER)
DONN'S WONDERFUL WAFFLES*
ASSORTED TOPPINGS
HOMEMADE SAUSAGE
FRENCH ROAST COFFEE

Apple Rings
4 Granny Smith apples
   or other green
   cooking apples
3 tablespoons butter
2 tablespoons
   granulated sugar

Wash and core apples (do not peel); cut into ⅜-inch-thick slices. In a large skillet, melt the butter and sauté apple slices until soft. Sprinkle the apple slices with sugar and continue cooking until sugar caramelizes. Serve hot. Makes 6 servings.

Donn's Wonderful Waffles
3 eggs, separated
1 cup sour cream
1 cup all-purpose flour
1 teaspoon baking
   soda
1½ cups buttermilk
5 tablespoons melted
   butter
Assorted toppings

Beat egg yolks until light. Mix in sour cream. Stir together flour and baking soda and mix into yolk mixture. Stir in buttermilk and melted butter, combining thoroughly.

Beat egg whites until soft peaks form and fold into batter. Bake in a Belgian (or other) waffle maker until golden and crisp. Serve with melted butter and Vermont maple syrup or fresh fruit in season, such as raspberries, sliced peaches, or sliced and lightly crushed strawberries. Makes 8 waffles.

MENU

CHAPPELLET CHENIN BLANC
•
SAUTÉED SHRIMP WITH SNOW PEAS
CHAPPELLET CHARDONNAY
•
PRITCHARD HILL POT PIES*
CHAPPELLET CABERNET SAUVIGNON
•
SALAD OF FINGER GREENS
•
PEARS-PLUM-YUM*

Pritchard Hill Pot Pies
2 tablespoons
   rendered bacon fat
1½ pounds each
   boneless lean lamb
   and beef, cut into
   1-inch cubes and
   dredged in flour
½ pound Polish
   sausages
1 cup Cabernet
   Sauvignon or other
   dry red wine
2 small onions, each
   stuck with 1 whole
   clove

2 medium-size
   carrots, cut into
   chunks
1 bay leaf, halved
2 sprigs each
   rosemary and thyme
2 cups each rich veal
   stock and rich
   chicken stock
2 teaspoons glace de
   viande
Salt and freshly
   ground black
   pepper to taste
10 baby carrots
10 pearl onions,
   blanched 5 minutes
3 turnips, cut into
   bite-size pieces
3 stalks celery with
   leaves, sliced ¼
   inch thick

A PRITCHARD HILL WINTER DINNER

½ cup Cognac
1 tablespoon butter
½ **pound fresh
mushrooms (wild,
if available), cut
into bite-size pieces**
3 shallots
2 cloves garlic,
chopped
1 small red bell
pepper, seeded and
coarsely chopped
2 small zucchini, cut
into bite-size pieces
5 kumquats, thinly
sliced and seeded
(optional)
½ cup chopped fresh
parsley
Flaky Pastry (recipe
follows)

In a large skillet, heat 1 tablespoon bacon fat and sauté lamb until browned, stirring meat constantly as it colors; remove lamb to a large saucepan. Add remaining tablespoon bacon fat to skillet and cook beef in the same manner; transfer to a second large saucepan. Sauté Polish sausages in fat remaining in skillet until browned; let cool, skin, slice 1 inch thick, and set aside. Deglaze skillet with wine, scrap-

ing up drippings, and divide evenly between beef and lamb. Add to each saucepan 1 onion and 1 cut-up carrot. Make a boquet garni for each pan by tying ½ bay leaf and 1 sprig each rosemary and thyme in a square of cheesecloth. Add 1 herb packet to each pot, along with enough water just to cover meats. Bring meats to a boil, cover, lower the heat, and simmer for 1¾ to 2 hours, or until meats are almost tender.

With a slotted spoon, lift meats from saucepans and put them together in a giant stockpot. Strain the cooking liquids, discarding herbs and vegetables, and combine them in a saucepan. Boil liquid to reduce to 1½ quarts, then pour over the meats in the stockpot. Add reserved sausage, veal stock, chicken stock, and glace de viande. Season with salt and pepper.

Bring meats to a boil, add baby carrots and pearl onions, reduce the heat, and simmer uncovered for 5 minutes. Add turnips,

celery, and Cognac and simmer for 5 minutes. In a skillet, melt the butter, add the mushrooms, shallots, and garlic and sauté until garlic is transparent, about 5 minutes. Add mushroom mixture to meats, along with bell pepper and zucchini.

Spoon an equal portion of the meat-vegetable mixture into each of 10 individual baking dishes, each with a capacity of about 1½ cups. Add a few kumquat slices to each dish, if desired, and then sprinkle each with a spoonful of parsley. Make pastry and roll out as directed. Top each dish with a pastry round, pressing the edges firmly against the rim of the dish and fluting them attractively. With a knife tip, make a small slit in each crust to allow steam to escape during baking. Bake pies in a preheated 425° F. oven for 10 minutes, or until crusts are golden brown and pies are heated through. Makes 10 servings.

Flaky Pastry This recipe will make enough pastry to cover 10 4-inch-in-diameter baking dishes. Place 4 cups all-purpose flour and 2 teaspoons salt in a mixing bowl. Add 1⅓ cups chilled shortening and cut into flour mixture with a pastry blender or 2 knives until mixture resembles coarse meal. Sprinkle ½ cup ice water over the surface, 1 tablespoon at a time, and mix lightly and quickly with a fork, just until pastry holds together. If pastry is too dry, add 1 or 2 additional tablespoons ice water. Shape pastry into a ball.

On a lightly floured board, roll dough out into a round no more than ⅛ inch thick. (You may want to divide the dough ball in half or thirds, depending on how large your work surface is.) Cut out 10 5-inch rounds and carefully transfer to the tops of the filled baking dishes. (If your dishes

are not exactly 4 inches across the top, cut out circles 1 inch larger than the diameter of the dishes you are using.)

Pears-Plum-Yum
10 Bosc or Anjou pears
**Lemon bath of 3
tablespoons fresh
lemon juice and 1
cup water**
**2 pounds Japanese
sour plums (see
Note)**
¼ **cup granulated
sugar, or to taste**
½ **cup water**

Peel pears, leaving on stems, and dip briefly in lemon bath. Refrigerate pears until serving time. In a saucepan, combine the plums,

sugar, and water and cook uncovered over medium heat until plums are tender. Remove from the heat and press plums through a food mill; discard skins and pits. Place pears upright on individual serving dishes and spoon some of the warm plum purée over them. Makes 10 servings. ***Note:*** *If plums are out of season, substitute puréed raspberry.*

Trefethen
VINEYARDS

NAPA VALLEY 1983
PINOT NOIR

GROWN, PRODUCED & BOTTLED BY
TREFETHEN VINEYARDS
NAPA, CALIFORNIA, U.S.A.
ALCOHOL 12.5% BY VOLUME

TREFETHEN VINEYARDS

Janet and John Trefethen, a young, dynamic couple, oversee six hundred acres of contiguous vineyards and the production of sixty thousand cases of award-winning varietals.

Both are third-generation Californians. "Grandma came over in a covered wagon in the gold rush of 1849," says vibrant, brown-eyed Janet. The daughter of a rice grower in the Sacramento Valley, she grew up "in rural America with the annual dove and duck hunts and wonderful picnics." From the age of three Janet rode and showed horses and became a California rodeo queen. "Someday I may make a quilt with the ribbons," she laughs. She was also on the women's ski team at the University of Nevada, where she earned a degree in journalism.

John was raised in Oakland and Piedmont, went to the University of North Carolina for a degree in comparative literature, and then enlisted in the navy. His parents purchased the run-down historic Eschol property, located in the southern end of Napa Valley, in 1968. At that time it was half prune trees and half vines that hadn't produced since 1940. Their intention was to farm it, growing and selling grapes to other wine makers.

Stanford University's master's program in business was John's next stop. At the time he didn't have an enormous interest in wine, but he wrote a report on operating a small

winery, which piqued his interest. When he graduated in 1972, he decided to try running the property along with a winery. Lacking a background in chemistry, he proceeded to the University of California's School of Oenology at Davis and took a concentrated course—"just enough to get through."

The Trefethens work with a young, enthusiastic staff, have a private plane, entertain a lot, and sleep with a hairtrigger frost alarm hanging over the bed. Their three-year-old son, Loren, adds further excitement to their lives.

Today they are winning international acclaim for their gold-medal

vintages and are busy with expansion. John has also just finished a term as president of the Napa Valley Vintners Association and both he and Janet are involved in the national marketing of their wines, working from spacious refurbished offices in their remodeled winery loft.

Janet's job includes considerable entertaining at home. In true Trefethen style, she serves guests vegetables from the garden and pies made with fruit from the orchard. "What I don't grow myself," she says, "I usually get down the road. The only thing that isn't local is rice from my father in Sacramento."

In summer and fall they often entertain around the pool. As the sun begins to slip behind the mountains, casting long purple shadows across the vineyards, their guests sip champagne from Schramsberg and Domaine Chandon, both made with Trefethen grapes.

Sometimes guests wander into the garden to help Janet pick tomatoes and arugula for the salad or choose nectarines from trees laden with fruit. John lights a fire on the outdoor grill, adding vineyard cuttings, and the aroma and the wine tantalize all.

MENU
Catered by Trump's Restaurant, Los Angeles

TRUMP'S SWORDFISH SALAD*
TREFETHEN CHARDONNAY

•

TRUMP'S ORIENTAL ROAST DUCK*
BLACK BEANS WITH WINTER SQUASH*
TREFETHEN PINOT NOIR

•

SELECTED CHEESES
TREFETHEN CABERNET SAUVIGNON

•

LEMON ICE CREAM
GINGERSNAPS

Trump's Swordfish Salad

1½ pounds swordfish steaks
1 teaspoon finely minced fresh ginger root
2 tablespoons fresh lime juice
½ clove garlic, minced
1 teaspoon chili oil
2 tablespoons peanut oil
½ teaspoon brown sugar
Ginger-Wine Vinaigrette (recipe follows)
4 cups assorted greens, such as radicchio, arugula, mâche, or butter lettuce
¼ pound enoki mushrooms
3 to 4 tablespoons salmon roe

Slice fish into ¼-inch-thick triangular-shaped slices. For the marinade, combine in a bowl the ginger root, lime juice, garlic, chili oil, peanut oil, and brown sugar. Add fish to bowl and marinate for a maximum of 2 hours. Prepare the Ginger-Wine Vinaigrette.

Remove fish from marinade and sear briefly in a skillet over high heat, or grill over a medium-hot fire for about 1 minute on each side. Meanwhile toss assorted greens with vinaigrette and spoon greens onto 6 plates. Arrange 3 slices of fish on top of each salad. Decorate with enoki mushrooms and salmon roe. Makes 6 servings.

Ginger-Wine Vinaigrette

In a jar with a tight-fitting lid, combine ½ teaspoon dry mustard, pinch each salt and granulated sugar, ¼ cup each olive oil and peanut oil, 3 tablespoons Chardonnay or other dry white wine, 1 tablespoon fresh lime juice, ⅛ teaspoon minced garlic, ¼ teaspoon chili oil, and ½ teaspoon minced fresh ginger root. Twist lid onto jar and shake well.

Trump's Oriental Roast Duck

½ cup soy sauce
2 tablespoons honey
2 tablespoons whole coriander seeds, crushed
2 ducklings (about 4 pounds each)

In a small saucepan, combine the soy, honey, and coriander seeds and heat to a low simmer, stirring to blend. Remove from the heat and pour into a vessel large enough to hold the ducks; cool. Put the ducks in the soy mixture and marinate for 4 hours.

Remove ducks from marinade, reserving marinade, and place on a rack in a roasting pan, breast sides down. Add hot water to pan to a depth of ¼ inch. Roast ducks in a pre-heated 400° F. oven for 30 minutes, turning twice. Reduce heat to 350° F. and roast 1 hour longer, or until legs move freely. Baste from time to time with liquid in pan. If ducks begin to brown too quickly, cover with foil to finish cooking.

Remove ducks to wooden board and let rest 20 minutes. To carve, cut off legs and thighs. Carve breasts by cutting down center of breastbone and then slicing meat against the rib cage. To serve, spoon Black Beans and Winter Squash (following) onto individual serving plates and arrange duck pieces on top, serving a leg or thigh and a portion of sliced breast to each diner. Brush duck pieces with some of the reserved marinade to form an attractive glaze. Makes 8 servings.

Black Beans and Winter Squash

2 cups dried black beans, rinsed (see Note)
2 tablespoons butter
2 medium-size onions, chopped
2 cloves garlic, minced
5⅓ cups chicken or duck stock
1 ham hock
2 bay leaves
Salt and freshly ground black pepper to taste
2 cups cooked winter squash, cut into ½-inch cubes
¾ cup whipping cream

Place beans in a saucepan, add water to cover, and bring to a boil. Boil 2 minutes, remove from the heat, and let stand for 1 hour; drain well.

In a large saucepan placed over medium heat, melt the butter, add onions, and sauté

for 5 minutes. Add 4 cups stock, ham hock, and bay leaves. Bring to a boil, lower the heat, cover, and simmer for 1½ to 2 hours, or until beans are tender. Do not overcook. Season with salt and pepper. If desired, the beans may be prepared to this point up to a day in advance. Cover and refrigerate until serving time.

To serve, place cooked beans in a large skillet with remaining 1⅓ cups stock, squash, and cream and bring to a boil. Boil until sauce is reduced to syrupy consistency. Makes 8 servings. **Note:** *Dried black beans, sometimes called turtle beans, are available in bulk in specialty markets.*

MENU

EMILY'S MEATBALL SOUP*

•

BROWN RICE BEAR BREAD*
TREFETHEN ESCHOL RED WINE
(for the big people)

•

HOMEMADE VANILLA ICE CREAM*
SUGAR COOKIES

Emily's Meatball Soup
1 pound ground round
3 tablespoons chopped onion
2 tablespoons fine fresh bread crumbs
1 clove garlic, minced
1 tablespoon finely chopped fresh parsley
1 egg
2 teaspoons water
1 tablespoon each chopped fresh oregano and chives
6 cups chicken stock (preferably homemade)
½ cup chopped fresh spinach
1 carrot, shredded
½ cup cooked long-grain white rice
Salt and freshly ground black pepper to taste

In a mixing bowl, combine the ground meat, onion, bread crumbs, garlic, parsley, egg, water, oregano, and chives. Mix thoroughly and roll into small balls. Pour stock into a large pot and heat to simmering. Slowly drop meatballs into simmering stock. Add spinach, carrots, and rice and simmer 6 to 8 minutes or until meatballs are cooked through. Season with salt and pepper. Ladle into bowls to serve. Makes 4 to 6 servings. **Note:** *For an adult crowd, add a few drops of Oriental-style sesame oil to soup and garnish with chopped fresh cilantro.*

Brown Rice Bear Bread
3½ to 4 cups unbleached flour
1 cup white cornmeal
2½ teaspoons salt
2 packages active dry yeast (scant 1 tablespoon each)
4 tablespoons butter, softened and cut into small pieces
2 cups tepid water (120° to 130° F.)
½ cup mild-flavored honey
2 cups cooked brown rice, at room temperature
1 egg, beaten

In a large mixing bowl, place 2 cups flour, cornmeal, salt, yeast, and butter. Gradually add water and honey to dry ingredients, mixing with electric beaters set at medium speed for 2 minutes. Scrape bowl sides occasionally as you beat. Add ½ cup flour and beat at high speed for 2 minutes. (Alternatively, combine the ingredients in manner described, but beat by hand with a wooden spoon. Each step will, of course, take longer.) Stir in rice and enough additional flour to make a soft dough. Turn dough out onto a lightly floured board and knead until smooth and elastic, about 5 minutes. Form dough into a rough ball, place in a lightly oiled bowl, and turn ball to oil top. Cover bowl and let dough rise in a warm place until doubled in volume, about 1 hour.

Punch down dough and turn out onto a lightly floured board. Divide in half. Cover and let rest 15 minutes. Now shape each half into a 9-inch round and place on a greased baking sheet. Cover and let rise in a warm place until doubled in volume. Using the handle of a long wooden spoon, make indentations in dough rounds at 1-inch intervals. Brush rounds with beaten egg. Bake in a preheated 375° F. oven for 30 to 35 minutes, or until loaves sound hollow when thumped. Remove from baking sheets and let cool on wire racks. Makes 2 loaves.

Homemade Vanilla Ice Cream
2 eggs
1 cup granulated sugar
Pinch salt
1½ tablespoons vanilla extract
2 cups milk
2 cups whipping cream

In a mixing bowl, combine the eggs and sugar and beat until light in color and mixture falls from spoon in a ribbon. Mix in salt, vanilla extract, milk, and cream, beating just until blended. Pour into an ice-cream freezer and freeze following manufacturer's instructions. Makes 6 servings, about 1½ quarts.

CLOS DU BOIS

1984

FLINTWOOD
Vineyard

DRY CREEK VALLEY
100% Chardonnay

PRODUCED & BOTTLED BY CLOS DU BOIS WINERY
HEALDSBURG, CALIFORNIA, U.S.A.   ALCOHOL 13.7% BY VOLUME

CLOS DU BOIS

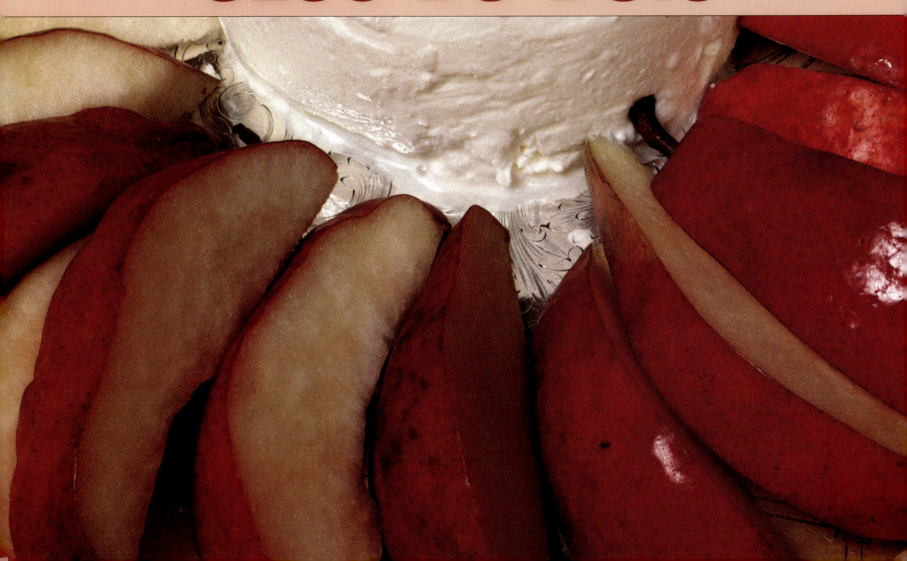

Southern specialties reign at the family and holiday tables of Kay and Frank Woods, who were both raised in the South. Frank hails from Tennessee, while Kay grew up in a small lumber town in Alabama and is still involved in her family's wood-products business.

Kay's father was an avid hunter and her mother a superb cook. As a youngster, Kay took her turn in spinning the duck press, stirring the currant sauce, and roasting, peeling, and grinding the chestnuts. A large part of her family life was centered around the preparation of fine meals.

Today the traditional holiday menus of the Woods family reflect this heritage, with their abundance of shrimp, crab, oysters, pecans, hot peppers, and wild game. Entertaining in their San Francisco home is often formal, with dinner parties for eight to twenty-four. At their century-old farm in Dry Creek, informality prevails.

There Kay cooks, using Sonoma County products: fresh vegetables from the garden, lamb and game birds from the region, chèvres from Laura Chenel, and fresh apple pies and berry tarts from Sebastopol. The whole atmosphere is very casual: guests pitch in to help cook, clean, and gather vegetables, herbs, and fruits.

"We bicycle along West Dry Creek and keep an eye on the spawning steelhead as they pass our vineyards," says Kay. The property was a farm when they purchased it and they still refer to it as their farm. The wood-frame ranch-style house has a large back porch that overlooks the vineyards. Here they savor wine or entertain at a table brightened by a freshly picked bouquet from the flower gardens that encircle the house.

As president of Clos du Bois, Frank oversees an award-winning winery that produces 250,000 cases a year. Naturally he is pleased when his wines win medals, and indeed, they tallied up more than any other winery in the country in both 1984 and 1985, according to *The Wine Spectator*. But Frank's primary goal is "to produce premium varietal wines that will add grace and pleasure to a good meal."

A congenial, buoyant person, Frank thinks that drinking wine is fun. His approach to running a winery is that of a consumer. "If I'm serving a wine I know," he says, "I anticipate how it will enhance the meal. If the wine is new, it's like an unopened present for which I have high hopes. In either case, a bottle of wine means a pleasant evening with good food and good friends."

A graduate of Cornell University's School of Hotel Administration, Frank joined the advertising department of Procter and Gamble, where he developed a mastery of marketing skills.

In the early 1970s he and two Cornell friends purchased several hundred acres, partly in fruit trees, in the Alexander and Dry Creek valleys of Sonoma County. Their studies indicated the land capable of becoming a fine vineyard. Frank furthered his education about the wine industry through courses and related work at the University of California, Davis.

In 1974 Frank and his partners made their first commercial quantity of wines bearing the Clos du Bois label. Since then, a sister winery, River Oaks, has evolved, producing reasonably priced bottlings that receive less cellar aging and are less complex.

The Woodses enjoy many family activities and travel extensively with their three children, Dorine, Frank Montgomery Woods III, and Alexis. They look forward to a yearly trip to Europe, and have been on safari in Africa, and on archeological "digs" in Spain, Kenya, and Italy. Ski trips to Colorado are high points, as are fishing trips to Montana or just taking their sailboat out on San Francisco Bay.

MENU

SAUTÉED SCALLOPS
CLOS DU BOIS BARREL FERMENTED
CHARDONNAY

•

HONEY LEMON DUCK*
SPOONBREAD*
BRAISED LEEKS
CLOS DU BOIS
FLINTWOOD CHARDONNAY

•

BELGIAN ENDIVE SALAD
CLOS DU BOIS
PROPRIETOR'S RESERVE
SAUVIGNON BLANC

•

MASCARPONE AND FRESH FRUIT
CLOS DU BOIS
LATE HARVEST GUWÜRZTRAMINER

Honey Lemon Duck

1 duckling with giblets (about 5 pounds)
Salt and freshly ground black pepper
2 cups water
1½ cups rich beef stock
½ cup dry white wine
3 lemons, quartered
1 cup raw honey
Peel from 3 lemons
1 cup water

Remove first 2 joints of the duck's wings and set aside. Remove pieces of loose fat from the cavity and reserve. Wash and wipe the cavity dry. Prick duck legs, back, and lower breast with a two-tine fork every ½ inch so that the fat beneath the skin will be released during cooking. Salt and pepper the duck's cavity and then truss. Place duck on a rack in a roasting pan, add 1 cup water to pan to prevent spattering, and set aside while sauce is prepared.

Heat a large skillet over medium heat with a small piece of the duck fat (or oil) and sauté the duck neck, gizzard, heart, and wing tips until browned. Add stock and wine, cover, and simmer over low heat for about 1 hour. Remove duck pieces from stock. Squeeze the juice from the lemon quarters into the stock, then add the quarters. Bring the stock to a boil, reduce the heat to a steady simmer, cook for 5 minutes, and strain. Add ½ cup honey, return to the heat, and simmer for 1 hour, or until reduced by one-half.

Meanwhile, cut the peel from 3 lemons (avoid any white membrane) into very fine julienne. In a saucepan, heat the water, add the remaining ½ cup honey, and simmer for 5 minutes. Add the peel to the pan and simmer until the peel is limp, about 15 to 20 minutes. Remove peel with a slotted spoon and set aside.

Place the duck, breast side down, preheated 400° F. oven for 30 minutes. Turn duck breast side up and reduce heat to 350° F. Roast the duck until the breast is medium done, but not dry, about 1 hour longer. Baste the duck with the sauce of sweetened stock the last 10 minutes of roasting.

Remove the duck from the roasting pan and carve each side of the breast into 4 slices. Place 2 breast slices and 1 leg or thigh on each of 4 plates. (Alternatively, quarter the duck.) Sprinkle glazed lemon peel over each serving. Pass the remaining sauce. Makes 4 servings.

Spoonbread

3 cups milk
1¼ cups white cornmeal
4 eggs
4 tablespoons butter, melted
2 teaspoons baking powder
½ teaspoon salt
Butter, for serving (optional)

In a large saucepan, bring milk to a boil over medium heat and immediately add the cornmeal. Cook, stirring constantly, until smooth and thickened. Remove from heat and cool. In a food processor fixed with a metal blade or in a mixing bowl, place the eggs, melted butter, baking powder, and salt. Spoon the cornmeal mixture around the blade of the food processor and process until creamy and thoroughly blended. Alternatively beat by hand until smooth and creamy.

Heavily butter a 2-quart ovenproof casserole and pour in the spoonbread mixture. Bake in a preheated 375° F. oven for 30 minutes. Serve from the casserole with a spoon. Accompany with butter, if desired. Makes 4 to 6 servings.

MENU

SANTA FE CHICKEN*
ORZO WITH ONIONS*
CHICORY SALAD*
CLOS DU BOIS GEWÜRZTRAMINER

•

SORBET

Santa Fe Chicken

- 2 whole chicken breasts, skinned and boned
- 1 tablespoon butter, or as needed
- 1 medium-size zucchini, grated and squeezed dry of moisture
- 2 jalapeño chili peppers, blanched 2 minutes, seeded, and chopped, or 1 can (4 ounces) chili peppers
- 1 clove garlic, minced
- ¾ cup whipping cream
- Salt and freshly ground black pepper to taste
- ½ cup toasted pine nuts

Cut chicken breasts into small fingers, as for a stir-fry. In a large skillet placed over medium-high heat, melt the butter and sauté chicken until opaque but not dry, about 5 minutes. Remove to a warm platter. In the same pan, sauté zucchini until it is free of moisture, about 2 minutes. Add chili peppers and garlic and sauté 1 minute. Return chicken pieces to pan and add cream. Simmer until heated through and cream is slightly reduced. Add salt and pepper and sprinkle with pine nuts. Makes 4 servings.

Orzo With Onions

- 2½ cups water
- ½ teaspoon salt
- 1 cup orzo (see Note)
- 1 small onion, chopped
- 2 tablespoons butter

In a large saucepan, bring water and salt to a boil, add orzo, and cook until al dente, about 10 to 15 minutes. Drain in a colander and toss to eliminate all water.

Meanwhile, melt the butter in a skillet, add onion, and sauté until golden brown, about 10 minutes. Add the drained orzo to the onion and heat, tossing, until orzo is coated with the butter and onion and heated through. Makes 4 servings. **Note:** *Orzo is a small, teardrop-shaped pasta.*

Chicory Salad

- 4 slices bacon (¼ inch thick), cubed
- 1 head chicory or curly endive
- 2 tablespoons balsamic vinegar or red-wine vinegar
- Freshly ground black pepper

Fry bacon in a large skillet until cooked, but not dry and crisp. Remove with a slotted spoon to a serving bowl. Pour off all but ¼ cup of the drippings. Tear chicory into bite-size pieces and place in bowl with the bacon. Reheat bacon drippings and add vinegar to deglaze the pan. Pour pan juices over the chicory and toss well. Pass pepper mill at the table. Makes 4 servings. **Note:** *Chicken livers may be used in place of the bacon. Cut 2 chicken livers into small pieces and sauté them in 1 tablespoon butter. Proceed as directed, adding ¼ cup olive oil to skillet before deglazing.*

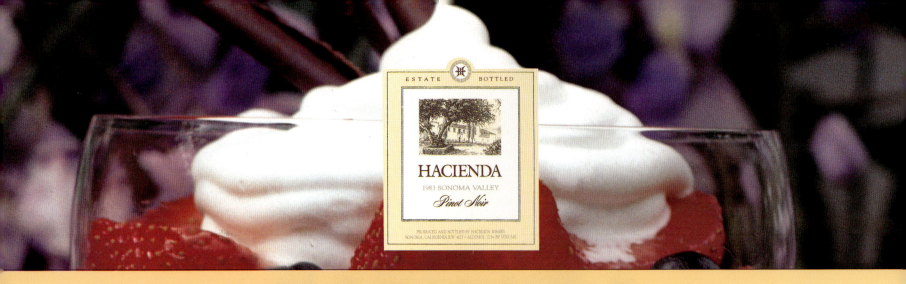

ESTATE BOTTLED

HACIENDA

1983 SONOMA VALLEY

Pinot Noir

PRODUCED AND BOTTLED BY HACIENDA WINERY
SONOMA, CALIFORNIA B.W. 4631 • ALCOHOL 12.5% BY VOLUME

HACIENDA WINE CELLARS

Nestled in a valley between rolling hills and majestic trees, Hacienda, a small, romantic winery in Sonoma Valley, stands on the land where European grape varieties were first commercially planted in California. The year was 1857. Count Agoston Haraszthy, a Hungarian nobleman, collected grape cuttings in France, Italy, Germany, and Spain and started the vineyards that surround Hacienda, now a Historic Landmark.

Haraszthy's vast vineyards fell into neglect until Frank Bartholomew, head of United Press International, took over the land in 1973 and transformed the old Sonoma Valley Hospital into Hacienda Wine Cellars. Following a career in investment banking, Crawford Cooley became owner and president in 1977.

A fifth-generation Californian, Crawford's ancestors arrived in the second overland party to the state, settling and planting grapes near Cloverdale in 1860. Today, he still oversees this twenty-one-thousand-acre property and a second ranch, and with the down-to-earth warmth and charm of a sophisticated rancher and successful businessman, he directs winery operations.

Steven MacRostie, a young, talented wine maker, is his partner. Steven believes great wines begin in the vineyard. He aims for elegant vintages with balance and has garnered awards for his work.

He shares with Crawford a unique talent for entertaining at the winery. This is a man's world, and the pair design great harvest feasts around "the fare from the Cooley Ranch in Cloverdale."

The nearby woods are home to deer and wild boar, and Crawford is a hunter. A Hacienda barbecue for seventy-five guests or more may feature spit-roasted or grilled venison, boar, and lamb, mixed green salad, raviolis, Sonoma French bread, and local cheese: Monterey Jack, dry Jack, and a choice of chèvres from Laura Chenel. Wine, cake, and fruit complete the feast.

The setting for a crowd is a grassy picnic spot under oak trees, overlooking a small lake and the old Haraszthy vineyard site. At other times the barrel room, with its naturally insulated fourteen-inch-thick brick walls, makes a cool retreat and festive locale.

Crawford grew up in the Bay Area where his father built a San Francisco law practice following graduation from Stanford University around the turn of the century. He served in the air force in the Second World War and returned to study economics at Stanford. Already a pragmatic businessman, he disputed the school's requirement for a foreign language and left in 1947 with all credits complete except Spanish.

He is a trustee emeritus of Stanford, president and trustee of the Filoli Center in Woodside, California, one of the great formal gardens of the United States, and president of the Marin County–based Agricultural Land Trust, an organization dedicated to balancing agricultural needs with urban sprawl. He and his wife, Jess, have four grown children; eldest son Robert serves as the national sales director of Hacienda. A champion cow-horse rider, Crawford now crisscrosses the United States on the wine circuit and breeds quarter horses on the side.

Wine maker Steven grew up in Sacramento and graduated from Whitman College in Washington, intending to go into medicine. A two-year stint with the army in Italy altered his plans, for it was there that he developed a passion for wine. After his discharge, he toured the wine-producing regions of Europe for six months and then entered the University of California, Davis and took a master's degree in oenology. He and his wife, Thale, have two young children.

MENU

CANTALOUPE WRAPPED IN
BLACK FOREST HAM
HACIENDA DRY CHENIN BLANC

•

GRILLED WILD BOAR*
HONEY-GLAZED CHESTNUTS*
RED CABBAGE COLE SLAW
CORN ON THE COB
HACIENDA PINOT NOIR

•

BERRY TRIO
WITH COINTREAU-FLAVORED CREAM*
HACIENDA GEWÜRZTRAMINER

Grilled Wild Boar

¼ cup olive oil
2 cloves garlic, chopped
2 teaspoons dried rosemary, crumbled
1 teaspoon salt
½ teaspoon freshly ground black pepper
1 cup dry white wine
1 boneless tenderloin of wild boar or domestic pork tenderloin (about 3 pounds)

For the marinade, mix together in a large bowl the oil, garlic, rosemary, salt, pepper, and wine. Add meat and marinate overnight. Insert a meat thermometer in the thickest portion of the tenderloin. Grill over a medium-hot mesquite fire in a covered barbecue for 45 minutes to 1 hour, or until thermometer registers 170° F. Makes 8 servings.

Honey-glazed Chestnuts

1 tablespoon honey
1 can (15 ounces) unsweetened whole chestnuts, drained

In a saucepan, heat honey and chestnuts over low heat, stirring until heated through and well coated. Makes 8 servings.

Berry Trio with Cointreau-flavored Cream

2 cups (1 pint) strawberries, sliced
2 cups (1 pint) raspberries
2 cups (1 pint) blueberries
5 tablespoons Cointreau or other orange-flavored liqueur
2 tablespoons granulated sugar
1 cup whipping cream
Semisweet chocolate curls for garnish

Combine strawberries, raspberries, and blueberries in a bowl. Spoon 3 tablespoons liqueur over berries and then sprinkle with 1½ tablespoons sugar; toss gently. Whip cream until stiff and fold in remaining 2 tablespoons liqueur and remaining 1½ teaspoons sugar. Spoon berries into dessert bowls. Top with cream and garnish with chocolate curls. Makes 8 servings.

MENU

SMOKED TROUT
HACIENDA SAUVIGNON BLANC

•

GAME BIRDS GRILLED ON MESQUITE*
WILD RICE WITH TOASTED WALNUTS*
ORANGE AND AVOCADO SALAD*
HACIENDA CHARDONNAY

•

STILTON
HACIENDA PORT

Game Birds Grilled on Mesquite

6 quail or doves, or
3 pigeons, dressed
½ cup olive oil
Juice of 3 lemons
(about 6 table-
spoons)
2 teaspoons butter,
melted
1 teaspoon dried
thyme or rosemary,
crumbled

Split birds along backbone and press breastbones firmly so that the birds are flat. Mix together the oil, lemon juice, butter, and thyme. Brush birds with oil mixture and place on grill, skin side down, over a medium-hot mesquite fire. Grill about 10 minutes for quail and doves and 30 minutes for pigeons, turning birds once and basting several times during cooking. Makes 6 servings.

Wild Rice with Toasted Walnuts

1½ cups wild rice
5 cups water
1½ teaspoons salt
2 tablespoons butter
¾ cup coarsely
chopped walnuts

Put wild rice in a strainer and wash well under cold running water. Place rice in a saucepan with water and salt, cover, and bring to a boil. Lower the heat and simmer for 30 minutes, or until just tender yet still chewy; drain. Toss rice with 1 tablespoon butter.

Meanwhile, sauté the walnuts in remaining 1 tablespoon butter until golden brown. Add to rice and mix gently. Makes 6 to 8 servings.

Orange and Avocado Salad

Lemon-Mustard
Vinaigrette (recipe
follows)
2 hearts of Romaine
lettuce
2 oranges, peeled and
sectioned
2 avocados, peeled,
pitted, and sliced
or diced

Prepare the Lemon-Mustard Vinaigrette. Break Romaine hearts into bite-size pieces and place in a salad bowl. Add orange sections. Pour the vinaigrette over the greens and oranges and mix gently. Add avocado and mix gently. Makes 6 servings.

Lemon-Mustard Vinaigrette

In a jar with a tight-fitting lid, combine ⅓ cup extra-virgin olive oil, 2 table-spoons fresh lemon juice, 2 teapoons Dijon-style mustard, and salt and freshly ground black pepper to taste. Twist lid onto jar and shake well.

Cakebread Cellars

NAPA VALLEY

Cabernet Sauvignon

1983

PRODUCED AND BOTTLED BY CAKEBREAD CELLARS
RUTHERFORD, NAPA VALLEY, CALIFORNIA, USA
ALCOHOL 12.5% BY VOLUME

CAKEBREAD CELLARS

Setting forth a bounteous harvest dinner comes naturally to Dolores Cakebread. Both she and husband Jack seem to thrive on challenges and juggling several jobs at once.

In their prize-winning redwood winery building in Rutherford, a festive repast is laid out with ease and simplicity. Likely it showcases the abundance of their spectacular vegetable garden, along with chicken and seafood dishes. Brilliant sunflower blossoms and purple artichoke flowers provide decor.

Throughout the several weeks of harvest, this pattern will be repeated daily. Friends will be invited to join the table and sample the winery's four varietals matched superbly to a bevy of dishes.

Cakebread Cellars is a second livelihood, or even a third, for the couple. A second-generation family garage business in Oakland, California, came first; and for Jack, photography is a professional side venture, with shows and assignments around the country.

It was 1973 when Jack was smitten by the wine industry, while on a photography assignment for Nathan Chronan's book, *The Treasury of American Wines.* Soon after, the Cakebreads casually approached longtime family friends about pur-

chasing their land in the heart of the valley, at Rutherford. Within weeks, Jack and Dolores were farmers in addition to running their garage.

Jack had tended almond orchards as a boy, so he was no stranger to

working the soil. Dolores remembers that on one of their first dates they spent the day harvesting almonds.

In the early days, they closed their Oakland shop each evening and then drove to the valley, where they planted twenty-two acres of Sauvignon Blanc by hand. "My job was pulling out all the morning glory and feeding the troops," says Dolores.

They started making wine in 1974. It was good wine, so they were encouraged to proceed.

During the building of the winery, friends would drop by on Saturdays to help and Dolores would provide a

huge buffet, toted fifty miles from her East Bay home.

At harvest time, the Cakebreads' three grown sons are on hand. Bruce, the youngest, is the full-time wine maker, having graduated in oenology from the University of California, Davis. Dennis and Steven both work away from the winery as accountants.

Dolores oversees the planting of the family vegetable patch where corn stands ten feet tall. Zucchini, crookneck squash, pumpkins, gourds, and melons flourish, and berries and lettuces provide prolific, never-ending crops.

She is also responsible for the flower garden that lines the drive. Its beauty automatically invites passers-by to stop. In autumn it is abloom with zinnias, yellow marigolds, and brown-eyed gloriosa daisies; in spring it is filled with tulips, daffodils, and assorted pansies.

"This has been an exciting project. We never planned it. The joy is meeting such happy people from all over the world. Those who enjoy food and wine are naturally neat people," says Dolores. "Life at the winery is quite a contrast to dealing with the unhappy customers who arrive at the garage with broken-down cars."

MENU

SHRIMP PUFFS*
CAKEBREAD CELLARS
SAUVIGNON BLANC

•

ITALIAN CHICKEN ROLL*
SLICED TOMATOES WITH BASIL AND
OIL-CURED OLIVES
GREEN BEAN BUNDLES VINAIGRETTE
CAKEBREAD CELLARS
CABERNET SAUVIGNON

•

CHOCOLATE TRUFFLES WITH
RASPBERRY PURÉE*
CAKEBREAD CELLARS CABERNET
SAUVIGNON

Shrimp Puffs

Puff Shells (see Basic Recipes)
1 cup small cooked shrimp, finely chopped
¼ cup fresh lime juice
3 ounces natural cream cheese, at room temperature
¼ cup whipping cream
2 tablespoons mayonnaise
Pinch salt
1 teaspoon Worcester-shire sauce
1 tablespoon minced green onion (white part only)
1 clove garlic, minced
1 teaspoon chopped fresh chives
2 dashes Tabasco sauce

Prepare the Puff Shells. In a bowl, marinate shrimp in lime juice at least 1 hour. In a mixing bowl, beat together cream cheese and cream until smooth and fluffy. Add mayonnaise and blend well.

Drain shrimp and stir into cheese mixture with salt, Worcestershire sauce, onion, garlic, chives, and Tabasco.

With a sharp knife, cut off the top one-third of each pastry shell to form a lid. Fill the shells with the shrimp-cheese mixture and replace tops. Serve at once. Makes about 30, 6 to 8 servings.

Italian Chicken Roll

1 chicken (about 2½ pounds)
Salt and freshly ground black pepper to taste
¼ pound baked ham, thinly sliced
⅓ cup toasted fine bread crumbs
¼ cup minced fresh parsley
1 teaspoon dried oregano, crumbled
15 soft, oil-cured black olives, pitted and sliced
¼ pound Genoa salami, thinly sliced
3 eggs, hard-cooked and halved
Dried oregano for coating
¼ pound sliced bacon
Tomato slices, fresh basil leaves, and oil-cured olives for garnish

Bone the chicken with poultry shears by cutting it down the back and removing rib cage and leg bones with the aid of a boning knife. Reserve wings, neck, giblets, and bones for stock. Spread the chicken, skin side down, on a sheet of plastic wrap and fold in the meat from the legs, spreading it over any bare skin and forming as even a layer of meat as possible. Sprinkle with salt and pepper. Arrange ham in a thin layer over chicken. In a bowl, mix together the bread crumbs, parsley, 1 teaspoon oregano, and pepper to taste. Sprinkle the ham with half the crumb mixture and spread the olives over the mixture. Arrange the salami over the olives and sprinkle with remaining crumb mixture. Place the egg halves lengthwise in a line down the center of the chicken.

Tuck in the ends of the chicken. Beginning at one of the long sides, roll the layered meats tightly around the eggs, using the plastic wrap as an aid in rolling. Holding the roll in place, tie it with kitchen twine at 1-inch intervals, making sure that the skin encloses all of the filling. Sprinkle the roll with oregano, salt, and pepper and place on a rack in a roasting pan. Cover the top of the chicken roll with bacon slices. Bake in a pre-heated 350° F. oven for 50 minutes, basting several times with the bacon drippings. Remove the bacon (reserve for another purpose), raise the oven heat to 425° F. and continue baking the chicken roll for 10 minutes, or until it is lightly browned. Let the roll cool to room temperature, wrap in plastic wrap, and chill overnight.

The next day, slice the roll ½ inch thick, arrange the slices on a platter, and let them stand at room tempera-ture for 1 hour. Garnish the platter with tomato slices topped with basil sprigs and oil-cured olives. Makes 6 to 8 servings.

Chocolate Truffles with Raspberry Purée

4 tablespoons unsalted butter
¾ cup whipping cream
1 tablespoon Grand Marnier
1 tablespoon Cabernet Sauvignon or other dry red wine
12 ounces bittersweet chocolate, finely grated
¼ cup unsweetened cocoa powder
2 packages (10 ounces each) frozen raspberries (un-sweetened or in a light syrup), thawed

In a saucepan placed over low heat, gently warm the butter and cream. Remove from the heat and stir in Grand Marnier and wine. Put grated chocolate in a bowl and pour butter mixture over it. With a whisk, whip until smooth and thick and soft peaks form. Cover and refrigerate at least 3 hours, or overnight.

To shape truffles, scoop balls from chocolate mixture with a melon baller. Drop balls onto a waxed-paper-lined baking sheet. Place in the freezer for 30 minutes to firm up. Remove truffles from the freezer and roll in cocoa powder. Refrigerate in a tin lined with plastic wrap for up to 24 hours before serving.

To serve, purée raspberries in a blender or a food processor fitted with a metal blade, then press purée through a sieve to remove seeds. Spoon a pool of raspberry purée on each plate and top with several truffles. Makes 6 to 8 servings.

MENU

**CHÈVRE AND WATER BISCUITS
CAKEBREAD CELLARS
SAUVIGNON BLANC**

•

**LOBSTER MEDALLIONS WITH TOMATO
SAFFRON SAUCE*
CAKEBREAD CELLARS CHARDONNAY**

•

**ROAST SQUAB WITH MUSHROOM–
SPAGHETTI SQUASH DRESSING*
FRESH VEGETABLES IN SEASON
CAKEBREAD CELLARS
CABERNET SAUVIGNON**

•

**SLICED PEARS WITH
BAVARIAN BLUE CHEESE
CAKEBREAD CELLARS
CABERNET SAUVIGNON**

Lobster Medallions with Tomato Saffron Sauce

**Tomato Saffron Sauce
   (see Basic Recipes)
4 lobster tails (4 to 6
   ounces each)
2 cups fish stock, or
   1½ cups bottled
   clam juice and ½
   cup dry white wine
1 English cucumber,
   peeled, if desired,
   and thinly sliced
2 tablespoons tobiko
   (see Note)**

Prepare the Tomato Saffron Sauce and set aside. In a large saucepan, poach lobster tails in stock for 10 minutes. Remove tails from stock, cool, and remove meat from shells, keeping tail meat in a single piece. Cut each tail into ¾- to 1-ounce medallions.

Select 8 individual white plates. Coat the bottom of each with an equal portion of Tomato Saffron Sauce and place 3 lobster medallions in a triangular shape in the center of each plate. Tuck 3 cucumber slices between the lobster medallions. Top the cucumber slices with dabs of tobiko. Makes 8 servings. **Note:** *Tobiko, Japanese flying fish roe, is available in Japanese fish markets.*

Roast Squab with Mushroom–Spaghetti Squash Dressing

**⅓ cup dried porcini
   mushrooms
Cabernet Sauvignon
   or other dry red
   wine
1 small spaghetti
   squash (about 1½
   pounds)
3 tablespoons butter
2 cloves garlic, minced
¼ pound fresh
   shiitake mushrooms
¼ pound fresh
   chanterelle
   mushrooms
¼ pound fresh button
   mushrooms
¼ cup sliced almonds
Salt and freshly
   ground black
   pepper to taste
8 boned squab
3 tablespoons
   raspberry vinegar
2 peeled cooked
   chestnuts, mashed**

In a bowl, soak porcini mushrooms in wine to cover just until plumped, about 30 minutes.

Make a few slits in squash with a knife to allow steam to escape during cooking and place squash in a baking pan. Bake in a preheated 350° F. oven for 1 hour, or until tender when pierced with a fork. Remove from the oven, allow to cool, cut in half, and remove seeds. With a fork, lift squash flesh out in spaghettilike strands and place in a bowl.

In a large skillet, melt 1½ tablespoons butter and sauté garlic 2 to 3 minutes. Drain porcini, reserving wine, and slice very thinly. Slice all the remaining mushrooms in the same manner. Add all of the mushrooms to the sautéed garlic and sauté briefly. Remove from the heat and transfer to a mixing bowl (do not wash the skillet). Let cool and add 2 cups of the squash. In a small skillet, heat almonds in 1½ teaspoons butter until lightly browned. Add to squash dressing and season with salt and pepper.

Spoon dressing into squab cavities, being careful not to pack it too tightly. Tuck neck and bottom skins around birds to form a nice plump shape. Place birds on a rack in a roasting pan and roast in a preheated 425° F. oven for 20 minutes, or until nicely browned.

While the squab are roasting, prepare the sauce. Deglaze the skillet in which the mushrooms were sautéed with raspberry vinegar and wine reserved from soaking mushrooms, plus additional wine as needed to measure 1 cup. Stir in chestnuts and whisk in remaining 1 tablespoon butter. Drizzle a little sauce over each bird just before serving. Makes 8 servings.

Louis M. Martini

1982
North Coast
Merlot

PRODUCED AND BOTTLED AT THE WINERY BY LOUIS M. MARTINI
ST. HELENA, NAPA VALLEY, CALIF., U.S.A.   BONDED WINERY 3596
ALCOHOL 12.5% BY VOLUME

LOUIS M. MARTINI WINERY

"The garden is my daily constitutional, and picking the berries a period of meditation," claims Elizabeth Martini, a serene, silver-haired woman and superb cook. As wife of Louis P. Martini and matriarch of the family winery, her warm personality and keen wisdom have played a vital, behind-the-scenes role in the operation of this third-generation family business.

Today three of their four children, Carolyn, Michael, and Patricia, carry the reins of one of California's first wineries, founded by their grandfather, Louis M. Martini, an Italian immigrant who helped his father peddle shellfish in San Francisco and vend homemade wine on the side.

In 1906 the nineteen-year-old Martini returned to his native country as an oenology student at the University of Genoa, where the professor advised, "If you want to make wine, better go back to California and experiment by yourself." He did just that and more, founding the winery in 1922. He was one of the first vintners to produce vintage varietal wines in quantity and helped revive viticulture after Prohibition.

Elizabeth bears a fascinating heritage as well. The fifth of eight children of Swiss-English parentage, she grew up in Santa Rosa, California. During the thirties she was expected to help with family chores, "and since I hated housework, I chose to cook for the family of ten instead."

In 1937 she attended the University of California, Berkeley, working her way through college in exchange for room and board and ten dollars a month. Her major was public health, but her therapy was cooking.

Each year she stayed with a different professor's family and her culinary horizons expanded to suit their tastes.

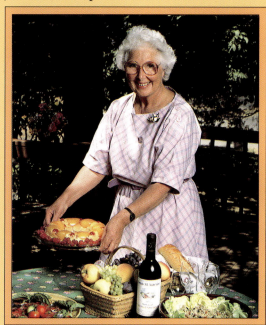

The first family, from New England, loved baked beans and brown bread; the second year all-American pies were in demand; her junior year, such continental pastries as *Dobosch Torte* were purchased from a Viennese bakery. As a college senior, she was a waitress at the Berkeley Women's City Club, a resident club, "and learned how it is done professionally."

Following graduation Elizabeth worked as a nutritionist. Though she and Louis attended Berkeley at the same time, they didn't meet and marry until later, when he returned from serving in the Second World War. Having trained in oenology and food technology at the University of California, he gradually assumed full responsibility for the wine making at his father's St. Helena winery.

Under his direction, the winery has reached its current annual production level of three hundred thousand cases, and the family has nearly doubled its original vineyard holdings to eight hundred acres in five separate locations in Napa and Sonoma counties.

Today Louis P. Martini continues to determine winery policy, leaving the wine making and cellar operations to his son, an oenologist trained at the University of California, Davis. The third generation is also represented by Michael's two sisters, Carolyn Martini, vice-president of sales and administration, and Patricia Martini, comptroller. Brother Peter, a film maker, has completed a documentary on the winery.

The many family occasions and entertaining demands offer ample opportunity for Elizabeth to be in her glory: experimenting in the kitchen. An orchard that yields persimmons, kiwi fruits, oranges, grapefruits, avocados, peaches, plums, quinces, and pears and an equally extensive vegetable garden provide her with much inspiration. "My grandmother had a family orchard in Healdsburg and I could close my eyes and smell the wonderful aroma of the ripening fruits," she says. "As the grocers kept bringing in sacks of green fruit, I planted my own trees."

She loves culinary challenges and rarely repeats recipes, "as they come from my head." She advises, "Louis always says, 'A meal is in balance when neither wine nor food overshadow each other.'"

MENU

SMOKED-SALMON SPREAD
WITH CRACKERS*
LOUIS M. MARTINI
SAUVIGNON BLANC OR SEMILLON

•

ROAST STUFFED LAMB*
STIR-FRIED SNOW PEAS
PILAFF
LOUIS M. MARTINI PINOT NOIR

•

TOSSED GREEN SALAD WITH PECANS
IN CABERNET DRESSING*
LOUIS M. MARTINI SPECIAL
SELECTION CABERNET SAUVIGNON

•

LIGHT AND DARK
CHOCOLATE-DIPPED STRAWBERRIES*

Smoked-Salmon Spread

½ pound cream cheese, at room temperature
¼ pound smoked salmon, chopped
2 teaspoons capers, drained
1 teaspoon chopped fresh dill, or ¼ teaspoon dried dill, crumbled
Fresh lemon juice to taste
Dill sprigs for garnish

Combine the cream cheese, salmon, capers, dill, and lemon juice in a blender or a food processor fitted with a metal blade. Blend to a smooth consistency. Spoon into a serving bowl, cover, and chill. Just before serving, garnish with dill sprigs. Makes about 1½ cups.

Roast Stuffed Lamb

¼ cup chopped onion
2 cloves garlic, minced
1 tablespoon olive oil
3 slices French bread, crusts removed and bread cubed
1 tablespoon minced fresh thyme, or ¾ teaspoon dried thyme, crumbled
Salt and freshly ground black pepper to taste
1 leg of lamb (4 to 5 pounds), boned
Mushroom Garnish (recipe follows)

In a skillet, sauté onion and garlic in oil until transparent, about 5 minutes. Place in a blender or a food processor fitted with a metal blade and add bread cubes, thyme, salt, and pepper. Whirl to a fine crumb consistency. Spoon the crumb mixture into the leg cavity from which the bone was removed, tie the leg closed with kitchen twine, and place on a rack in a roasting pan. Season meat with salt and pepper. Insert a meat thermometer into the thickest portion of the leg. Roast in a preheated 400° F. oven for 20 minutes; reduce the heat to 325° F. and roast about 1 hour longer, allowing 20 minutes to the pound or until thermometer registers 145° F. for medium-rare.

When the lamb goes in the oven, prepare the Mushroom Garnish. To serve, place lamb on a serving board and arrange the stuffed mushroom caps alongside. Makes 8 servings.

Mushroom Garnish

Pull stems from 16 medium-size (1½ inches in diameter) mushrooms and set stems aside. Dip caps in fresh lemon juice and then place them, stem side up, in a greased baking dish. Combine the reserved stems, 2 slices French bread, crusts removed and bread cubed, 1 tablespoon mayonnaise, 2 tablespoons freshly grated Parmesan cheese, and 1 clove garlic, minced, in a blender or a food processor fitted with a metal blade. Whirl to a fine crumb consistency. Fill the caps with the crumb mixture and put them into the 325° F. oven with the lamb the last 40 minutes of roasting.

Tossed Green Salad with Pecans in Cabernet Dressing

Cabernet Dressing (recipe follows)
2 or more heads assorted greens, such as curly endive, radicchio, butter lettuce, or red oak-leaf lettuce
⅓ cup coarsely chopped toasted pecans
6 ounces Bavarian blue cheese (optional)

Prepare the Cabernet Dressing. Tear greens into bite-size pieces and place in a large bowl. Pour dressing over greens and mix lightly. Sprinkle dressed greens with pecans, and serve with squares of blue cheese, if desired. Makes 8 servings.

Cabernet Dressing

In a jar with a tight-fitting lid, combine ½ cup olive oil, ¼ cup each Cabernet Sauvig-

non and fresh lemon juice, ¼ teaspoon Dijon-style mustard, 2 or 3 fresh basil leaves, chopped, and salt and freshly ground black pepper to taste. Twist lid onto jar and shake well.

Light and Dark Chocolate-dipped Strawberries

4 ounces semisweet chocolate, chopped
4 ounces white chocolate chips
4 cups (2 pints) large strawberries

Place semisweet chocolate and white chocolate in separate small bowls and melt over simmering water, stirring until smooth. Pat berries clean with paper towels. Holding each berry by the stem end, dip half of the berries in dark chocolate and half of them in white chocolate, coating just the bottom half of each berry. Place on a foil-lined baking sheet to cool and firm up. Serve on a platter or individual plates. Makes 8 servings.

MENU

SLICED TOMATOES VINAIGRETTE
POACHED CHICKEN BREASTS WITH
BLACKBERRY CABERNET SAUCE*
TABBOULEH SALAD*
LOUIS M. MARTINI
CABERNET SAUVIGNON
LOUIS M. MARTINI CHARDONNAY

•

PEACHES POACHED IN WINE

Poached Chicken Breasts with Blackberry Cabernet Sauce
2 cups water
1 cup dry white wine
1 bay leaf
1 slice onion, coarsely chopped
1 carrot, coarsely chopped
Leaves from 1 stalk celery, chopped
½ teaspoon salt
¼ teaspoon freshly ground black pepper
6 chicken breast halves (2 to 2½ pounds)
Blackberry Cabernet Sauce (recipe follows)

In a large pot, combine the water, wine, bay leaf, onion, carrot, celery leaves, salt, and pepper. Bring to a boil over medium heat and boil 5 minutes. Add chicken pieces, bring back to a boil, cover, reduce the heat to low, and simmer 15 minutes. Turn off heat and let pot stand, covered, until cool. Lift chicken pieces from cooking stock with a slotted utensil. Skin and bone the breast halves and slice thinly lengthwise, holding them in their original shape as you work. Arrange the sliced breasts on a platter, cover with plastic wrap, and chill. (Strain the stock and reserve for use in other dishes.)

Prepare Blackberry Cabernet Sauce and spoon over chilled chicken just before serving. Makes 6 servings.

Blackberry Cabernet Sauce Purée and then strain enough blackberries to measure 1 cup pulp (about 2 cups berries). In a skillet, sauté 1 small onion, chopped, in 3 tablespoons safflower oil until transparent, about 5 minutes. Add the berry pulp to the onions along with 3 tablespoons granulated sugar and 1 cup Cabernet Sauvignon. Simmer sauce until reduced to desired consistency, approximately half the original quantity. Let cool, then chill. This sauce is also good with turkey, duck, or pork.

Tabbouleh Salad
1 cup finely ground bulghur wheat
2 cups water
2 tablespoons olive oil
½ cup Mediterranean-style olives, pitted and halved
½ cup chopped fresh parsley
2 or 3 fresh basil leaves, chopped
1 small red bell pepper, seeded and chopped
½ cup coarsely chopped toasted pecans or walnuts
2 tablespoons minced green onion
Juice of 1 lemon (about 2 table-spoons)
Salt and freshly ground black pepper to taste
Romaine lettuce leaves

Put bulghur wheat in a deep bowl. Bring water to a boil, pour it over the bulghur, and let bulghur stand 1 hour. Drain bulghur well and return it to the bowl. Add the oil, olives, parsley, basil, red pepper, pecans, onion, lemon juice, salt, and black pepper; mix lightly. Cover and refrigerate 2 to 3 hours.

To serve, spoon onto a lettuce-lined platter, or mound in a serving bowl with Romaine leaves tucked down along the sides of the bowl. Makes 6 servings.

Schramsberg

CUVÉE DE PINOT

NAPA VALLEY
CHAMPAGNE

VINTAGE 1983
PINOT NOIR

PRODUCED AND BOTTLED BY
SCHRAMSBERG VINEYARDS
CALISTOGA, CALIFORNIA

ALCOHOL 12% BY VOLUME
CONTENTS 750 MLS

SCHRAMSBERG VINEYARDS

Jack and Jamie Davies are contemporary pioneers. As owners of Schramsberg Vineyards, they are credited with revolutionizing the sparkling wine industry in America.

Their tale begins with a gamble in 1965 and brims with dauntless determination, incessant labor, and financial hardship. The turning point was 1974. That year President Nixon took Schramsberg 1969 Blanc de Blancs to China to toast a new era in Chinese-American relations, and the California sparkling wine made news worldwide.

As they celebrated their twentieth harvest in 1985, they radiated success. Their first vintage was 250 cases; the current annual production is fifty thousand cases, though these wines will not be ready for release for another three or more years.

Schramsberg wines have been served on more state occasions than any other California sparkling wine. The last four American presidents have toasted numerous heads of state with Schramsberg vintages, including Queen Elizabeth, Emperor Hirohito of Japan, and the presidents of France and Mexico.

In the sixties, Jack and Jamie left a comfortable corporate life in the city and moved, with young children, to the run-down one-hundred-year-old winery and sprawling Victorian home once owned by Jacob Schram. A German immigrant and barber turned wine maker, Schram had hired Chinese coolies to dig the once-famous underground cellars that were a century later all but forgotten on the Mount Diamond property south of Calistoga.

Jack had quit a promising marketing career as vice-president for an industrial corporation and Jamie had sold her art gallery. They gave up all

to move into the derelict home and commence a daring goal of producing a sparkling wine as close to the French prototype as was possible on California soil.

"Friends and family thought we had acquired a white elephant and were zany besides," says Jamie, relaxing in their beautifully crafted new winery office. But there was a good reason for their life-style switch.

"We wanted to test out a lot of ideas: that creativity exists," she explains. "You can take artistry and create and add a new dimension to your life. We were looking for an opportunity to do something on our own. Starting with growing something was appealing to us. Finding a rural environment was also important."

The Davieses were not, however, complete novices on the subject of wineries. They were already shareholders in Mt. Eden Vineyards and had spent many weekends working the crush and reading and studying about wine.

In those early years they did everything, including replant forty acres of vineyard. Jack was the exclusive wine maker for seven years, with Dimitri Tchelistcheff, a warm and encouraging consulting oenologist.

Today Schramsberg produces four styles of sparkling wine and a Reserve from special lots that get longer aging on the yeasts. The size of the tunnels, or underground cellars, has been tripled and the wine-making facility has undergone a major expansion. A new vacuum system of Jack's own invention conveys the grapes from waiting delivery trucks to the presses, minimizing damage to the grape skins.

Once the Davieses carved out a niche with sparkling wine, they embarked on a new venture, another first: producing a Cognac-style brandy in California. They formed a joint partnership with Remy Martin and their first brandy was ready in 1985.

"We've been lucky to be in an environment with an extraordinary group of people who have enhanced our lives," says Jamie. "We have the science, the climate, and a lot of talented people who have given a lot of support and a lot of sharing of techniques.

SCHRAMSBERG VINEYARDS: A SUMMER LUNCH ON THE VERANDA

MENU

GOUGÈRE WITH CHÈVRE*
SCHRAMSBERG BLANC DE BLANCS
CHAMPAGNE

•

MUSHROOM TART*
SCHRAMSBERG CUVÉE DE PINOT
CHAMPAGNE

•

SCHRAMSBERG CHICKEN*
TINY GREEN BEANS
SCHRAMSBERG BLANC DE NOIRS
CHAMPAGNE

•

HOT ORANGES AND BERRIES
CREMANT*
BUTTER COOKIES
SCHRAMSBERG CREMANT DEMI SEC

Gougère with Chèvre

1¼ cups water
¼ pound (½ cup) butter, cut into small pieces
½ teaspoon salt
½ teaspoon freshly ground black pepper
1¼ cups all-purpose flour
5 eggs
½ pound firm chèvre, such as Montrachet, diced
Egg white, lightly beaten, for glaze

In a large saucepan, bring the water to a boil. Add butter, salt, and pepper. Return to a boil, remove from the heat, and add flour all at once, mixing well with a wooden spoon. Return pan to low heat and cook, stirring, until mixture pulls away from the sides of the pan and forms a ball. Remove from heat. Add eggs, one at a time, mixing thoroughly after each addition. Set aside 2 tablespoons diced cheese and mix remaining cheese into the paste.

Pack dough into a pastry bag fitted with a star tube. On a greased baking sheet, press out 2- to 3-inch mounds to form a ring about 10 inches in diameter. The center of the ring should be about 3 to 4 inches in diameter. Now press out remaining one-third of dough in smaller mounds atop the first layer, positioning them in interstices between the mounds. Brush ring with egg white and scatter reserved cheese on top. Bake in a preheated 375° F. oven for 40 minutes, or until puffed and golden brown. Serve hot, cut into wedges. Makes 8 servings.

Mushroom Tart

Partially Baked Quiche Shell (see Basic Recipes)
6 slices bacon, finely diced
3 tablespoons olive oil
1 pound mushrooms (preferably a combination of domestic and wild), thinly sliced
2 cloves garlic, minced
2 tablespoons minced fresh parsley
½ teaspoon dried tarragon, crumbled
4 eggs
1 cup milk or half-and-half
1 cup freshly grated Parmesan or Asiago cheese
¼ teaspoon each salt and freshly ground black pepper

Prepare the Partially Baked Quiche Shell. In a large skillet, cook bacon until crisp; remove from pan with a slotted utensil and drain on paper towels. Discard bacon drippings. In the same skillet, heat the oil and sauté mushrooms for 2 minutes, or until soft. Add garlic, parsley, and tarragon and remove from the heat; cool to room temperature. Beat eggs until light and stir in milk, mushroom mixture, cheese, reserved bacon, salt, and pepper. Pour into prepared quiche shell. Bake in a preheated 350° F. oven for 25 to 30 minutes, or until set. Serve warm or at room temperature, cut into wedges. Makes 8 servings.

Schramsberg Chicken

2 tablespoons butter
1 tablespoon olive oil
2 fryer chickens (about 3½ pounds each)
2½ cups Blanc de Noirs Champagne
Bouquet garni of 2 sprigs parsley, 1 small sprig thyme, and 1 bay leaf
2 tablespoons chopped fresh tarragon, or 1 teaspoon dried tarragon, crumbled
¼ teaspoon each salt and freshly ground black pepper
2 cups whipping cream
Fresh herbs, such as tarragon, thyme, and parsley, for garnish
Nasturtium blossoms for garnish

In a large skillet, heat the butter and oil and sauté chickens until lightly browned on all sides. Transfer to a flameproof casserole and pour in Champagne. Enclose bouquet garni herbs in a square of cheesecloth and secure with kitchen twine. Add to casserole along with 1 tablespoon tarragon, salt, and pepper. Cover, bring to a simmer (do not allow to boil), and

cook for 40 to 45 minutes. Remove from the heat and let chickens cool in the liquid.

When cool, remove chickens from the liquid, remove and discard the skin, and cut chickens into meaty serving pieces. Arrange pieces on a platter, cover with plastic wrap, and refrigerate. Strain cooking liquid into a large saucepan and boil to reduce by one-half. Remove from the heat and stir in cream. Return pan to the heat and cook the sauce, stirring constantly, until it thickens, about 5 to 8 minutes. Remove from the heat, cool to room temperature, and stir in remaining 1 tablespoon tarragon. Spoon sauce over chicken and garnish with fresh herbs and nasturtium blossoms. If desired, cook chicken and make sauce 24 hours in advance, then combine just before serving. Makes 8 servings.

SCHRAMSBERG VINEYARDS: AN AUTUMN DINNER

MENU

SEA BASS IN PARCHMENT WITH
LEEKS AND GINGER*
SCHRAMSBERG BLANC DE NOIRS
CHAMPAGNE

•

GRILLED QUAIL*
SPOONBREAD
SAUTÉED MUSHROOMS
CUVÉE DE PINOT CHAMPAGNE

•

WATERCRESS SALAD*

•

CALISTOGA APPLE TORTE*
SCHRAMSBERG CREMANT DEMI SEC

Hot Oranges and Berries Cremant

3 tablespoons butter
¼ cup firmly packed brown sugar
3 tablespoons thawed undiluted orange juice concentrate
½ cup Cremant Demi Sec
6 oranges, peeled and sliced crosswise
2 cups hulled strawberries, halved
1 cup blueberries
3 tablespoons sliced toasted almonds (optional)

In a large skillet, combine the butter, sugar, and orange concentrate and simmer for 5 minutes. Blend in Champagne, add orange slices, and heat through. Serve hot orange slices and the Champagne sauce on dessert plates and scatter over strawberries and blueberries. Sprinkle with toasted almonds, if desired. Makes 6 to 8 servings.

Sea Bass in Parchment with Leeks and Ginger

3 or 4 medium-size leeks
6 tablespoons butter
3 slices fresh ginger root, cut into thin julienne
½ cup Blanc de Noirs Champagne
2 carrots, cut into julienne
1 red bell pepper, cut into julienne
3 green onion tops, cut into julienne
Salt and freshly ground black pepper to taste
6 sea bass fillets (4-ounce fillets cut 1 inch thick)

Split leeks lengthwise, wash well under cold running water, and cut white part and some of the green into julienne. In a skillet, melt butter and sauté leeks until wilted, about 5 minutes. Add ginger and Champagne. Cook briskly until liquid evaporates. Remove from the heat and set aside to cool.

Cut cooking parchment into 16-by-24-inch pieces. Fold each piece in half crosswise and cut out to form heart shape. Open hearts flat and place one-sixth of the leek mixture on one-half of each heart, leaving a 1-inch border. Top with one-sixth of the carrots, bell pepper, and onion tops. Place a fish fillet on top of each portion of vegetables. Season lightly with salt and pepper.

Fold heart over fish and form small pleats around open side to seal edges together. Place packets on baking sheets and bake in a preheated 400° F. oven for 5 to 6 minutes, or until packets puff and start to brown. Serve at once; let guests open packets at the table. Makes 6 servings.

Grilled Quail

12 quail
Olive oil
3 cups coarsely chopped mixed fresh herbs, such as rosemary, sage, parsley, and thyme
Balsamic vinegar

Rub quail inside and out with olive oil. Stuff each quail with ¼ cup of the herb combination and truss the birds. Place quail over a medium-hot mesquite fire and grill, turning, about 10 minutes, or until well browned on all sides. Brush birds *lightly* with olive oil during cooking; avoid using too much oil or high flames will result. Place quail on a serving dish and drizzle lightly with balsamic vinegar. Makes 6 servings.

Watercress Salad

½ pound mung bean sprouts
½ pound snow peas
4 green onions
2 bunches watercress, stems removed
⅓ cup olive oil
2 tablespoons rice-wine vinegar
1 teaspoon Oriental-style sesame oil
Salt and freshly ground black pepper to taste

Immerse bean sprouts in boiling water for 30 seconds; drain, rinse under cold running water, and drain again. "String" peas and immerse in boiling water for 1 minute; drain, rinse under cold running water, and drain again. Cut snow peas into 1-inch pieces on the diagonal. Chop green onions, including some of the green tops. Coarsely chop watercress and put in a serving bowl along with bean sprouts, snow peas, and green onions. Mix together olive oil, vinegar, sesame oil, salt, and pepper. Pour dressing over vegetables, adding only enough to moisten lightly, and mix gently. Makes 6 servings.

Calistoga Apple Torte

2 eggs
1 cup firmly packed brown sugar
¼ cup all-purpose flour
2½ teaspoons baking powder
Pinch salt
2 teaspoons vanilla extract
1 cup coarsely chopped walnuts, pecans, or almonds
1½ cups coarsely chopped peeled and cored apples
Whipped cream flavored with confectioners' sugar and ground cinnamon

In a mixing bowl, beat together eggs and brown sugar until light. Stir in flour, baking powder, salt, and vanilla extract. Add nuts and apples and pour into a greased 9-inch pie pan. Bake in a preheated 350° F. oven for 30 minutes, or until golden brown. Cut into wedges and serve warm with whipped cream flavored with confectioners' sugar and cinnamon. Makes 8 servings.

BASIC RECIPES

BASIC RECIPES

Beef Stock

3 to 4 pounds meaty beef bones
2 onions, chopped
2 cloves garlic
1 carrot, chopped
1 stalk celery, chopped
Few celery leaves
Bouquet garni of
  3 sprigs parsley,
  2 sprigs thyme, and
  1 bay leaf tied in
  a cheesecloth bag
2 cloves garlic
2 teaspoons salt

Place bones in a roasting pan and roast in a preheated 450° F. oven for 20 minutes, or until browned. Transfer bones to a soup kettle. Add onions, garlic, carrot, and celery stalk and leaves. Tie herbs for bouquet garni in a square of cheesecloth and add to the pot. Pour in water to cover and add salt. Bring to a boil, skim off any foam that forms on surface, lower the heat, and simmer partially covered for 3 to 4 hours, skimming off foam from time to time. Add additional water as needed to keep bones covered. Strain stock, then refrigerate or freeze until needed. Before using, lift off and discard fat that solidifies on top. Makes about 2 quarts.

Veal Stock
Substitute veal bones for the beef bones in Beef Stock. Proceed as directed.

Duck Stock
Substitute duck bones for the beef bones in Beef stock. Proceed as directed.

Chicken Stock

3 to 4 pounds chicken necks and wings
2 quarts water
1½ teaspoons salt
1 onion, quartered
1 stalk celery, sliced
1 carrot, peeled and halved

In a soup kettle, combine the chicken necks and wings, water, salt, onion, celery, and carrot. Bring to a boil, skim off any foam that forms on surface, lower the heat and simmer partially covered for 1½ hours. Strain stock, then refrigerate or freeze until needed. Before using, lift off and discard fat that solidifies on top. Makes about 1½ quarts.

Chocolate Cups
Melt 6 ounces semi-sweet chocolate chips in the top pan of a double boiler placed over simmering water. Using a spatula, spread the warm melted chocolate in a thin layer over the bottom and sides of 6 paper cupcake liners. Cool in the refrigerator. When chocolate is hard, carefully pull the paper away from the cups.

Demi-Glace
This sauce begins with a long-simmered brown meat sauce: beef, veal, or duck stock simmered and skimmed for several hours until it is reduced to a thick sauce that coats the back of a spoon. Start with one of these basic stocks, but double or triple the recipe depending on quantity desired, as 2 quarts of stock will reduce down to about ⅓ to ½ cup of demi-glace. Allow at least 12 hours to achieve this process.

Dorée Sauce
Mix together 1 cup homemade mayonnaise, 1 tablespoon Sherry vinegar, 1 tablespoon tomato paste, and a dash of Cognac.

Fish Stock

1½ to 2 pounds fish bones and heads
1½ quarts water
2 cups dry white wine or dry vermouth

1 tablespoon chopped
fresh thyme, or
¾ teaspoon dried
thyme, crumbled
2 onions, stuck with
2 whole cloves
2 carrots, diced
2 cloves garlic
1 bay leaf
1½ teaspoons salt
4 peppercorns

In a large soup pot, combine fish parts and water, bring to a boil, lower the heat, and simmer partially covered for 30 minutes. Strain through a fine sieve. Return stock to pot and add wine, thyme, onions, carrots, garlic, bay leaf, salt, and peppercorns. Bring to a boil and simmer partially covered for 20 minutes. Strain and refrigerate or freeze. Makes about 1¾ quarts.

Glace De Viande

This meat glaze is prepared from a demi-glace boiled and reduced to a syrup that becomes a firm jelly when it is cold.

Mayonnaise

1 whole egg, or 2 egg
yolks
1 tablespoon fresh
lemon juice or
vinegar
½ teaspoon salt

½ teaspoon dry
mustard
¼ teaspoon freshly
ground black
pepper
1 cup safflower oil

In a blender or a food processor fitted with a metal blade, combine the egg, lemon juice, salt, mustard, and pepper. Blend a few seconds. With motor running, gradually pour in oil in a slow, steady stream, blending until smooth and thickened. Turn into a container, cover, and chill. Makes about 1 cup.

Partially Baked Quiche Shell

Place 1½ cups all-purpose flour into a food processor fitted with a metal blade, or into the bowl of an electric mixer. Cut ¼ pound butter into small cubes. Add the butter to the flour and mix briefly until crumbly. Add 1 egg yolk and about 3 tablespoons cold water, and mix until dough pulls away from sides of processor bowl and is pliable enough to shape into a ball. (If the dough remains crumbly, add a little more water.) Wrap dough ball in

waxed paper and chill briefly. Roll out dough on a lightly floured board into a 12-inch circle. Drape circle around rolling pin and center over an 11-inch quiche pan. Carefully ease dough into pan, pressing it firmly against the bottom and sides and attractively fluting the edges. Line pastry-lined pan with aluminum foil, fill with pie weights or dried beans to hold dough in place, and bake in a preheated 425° F. oven for 8 minutes. Remove weights and foil and let shell cool before filling.

Puff Shells

In a saucepan, melt 4 tablespoons butter in ½ cup boiling water. Stir together ½ cup all-purpose flour and ¼ teaspoon salt and add to the hot mixture all at once, stirring constantly. Cook until mixture leaves the sides of the pan and forms a smooth ball. Remove from heat and cool 1 minute. Add 2 eggs, one at a time, beating thoroughly after each addition until mixture is smooth again. Drop by rounded ½ teaspoonfuls onto greased baking sheets,

making about 30 mounds in all. Bake in a preheated 450° F. oven for 7 minutes, or until tops begin to brown; reduce heat to 400° F. and bake 10 to 12 minutes longer, or until puffed, golden brown, and crisp. Let cool on a wire rack.

Red Pepper Sauce

Sear 2 red bell peppers over an open flame until blackened, or char in the broiler. Place peppers in a closed brown-paper bag for 10 minutes so that they "sweat," then remove from the bag and peel away black skin. (Peeled roasted peppers are available in jars and may be substituted.) Split peppers open, discard seeds, and place peppers in a blender or a food processor fitted with a metal blade. Add 2 tablespoons raspberry vinegar and 2 tablespoons extra-virgin olive oil and purée until smooth. Season with salt and freshly ground black pepper and refrigerate until ready to serve.

Sabayon Sauce

In a mixing bowl, beat together 3 egg yolks

and ⅓ cup granulated sugar until mixture falls from a spoon in a ribbon. Transfer to the top pan of a double boiler placed over simmering water and whisk in ¾ cup Gewürztraminer; continue to beat until mixture is nearly tripled in volume and thickened. Remove from the heat and nest pan in a bowl of ice. Whisk sauce until cool, then chill.

Tomato Saffron Sauce

In a skillet placed over medium heat, melt 1 tablespoon butter and sauté 2 shallots, finely chopped, for 5 to 7 minutes. Add 2 teaspoons chopped fresh tarragon (or ½ teaspoon dried tarragon, crumbled), ⅛ teaspoon ground white pepper, ¾ cup fish stock or bottled clam juice, pinch powdered saffron, and ¾ cup Chardonnay or other dry white wine. Boil mixture to reduce to about ½ cup. Stir in 1½ tablespoons tomato paste, mixing well. Strain through a fine sieve into a mixing bowl. Stir in 1 cup mayonnaise. Add ¾ teaspoon fresh lemon

juice, salt and freshly ground black pepper to taste, and a dash of Tabasco sauce.

Truffles

Melt together in the top pan of a double boiler placed over simmering water 7 ounces semisweet chocolate and 1 ounce unsweetened chocolate. Add 4 tablespoons each salted and unsalted butter and 2 tablespoons whipping cream. Stir until thoroughly blended. Cool mixture and refrigerate until it is firm and easily holds its shape, about 30 minutes.

With a melon baller, scoop chilled mixture into ⅜" balls. Place balls in a tin lined with plastic wrap, cover, and refrigerate until serving time.

Vinaigrette

Mix together 1 teaspoon Dijon-style mustard, 3 tablespoons olive oil, and 1 tablespoon balsamic vinegar until well blended.

RECIPE INDEX

INDEX

INDEX

INDEX

INDEX

INDEX